Praise for **Stop Second-Guessing Yourself—The Preschool Years**

"Thank goodness for Jen Singer: She'll talk you down off the ledge of parenting, then make you laugh and actually enjoy this crazy time."
—Sarah Smith, senior editor, *Parenting* magazine

"For mothers wondering whether they're the only ones who find birthday parties a nightmare and getting out the door impossible, *Stop Second-Guessing Yourself* is a lifeline. Jen Singer weaves together pages and pages of practical advice, funny stories, and insights. Her mixture of humor, reality and compassion will give all moms a lift."
—Kate Kelly, managing editor, *American Baby*

"Jen Singer's books are full of great advice to help moms conquer the toughest job in town—parenting. In fact, she's been my own 'potty whisperer'! They say it takes a village to raise a child, but Jen has managed to gather all the town's mothers and pass along great advice for us all."
—Melissa Joan Hart, actress

"Jen Singer gets it! Finally—someone who truly understands what parents of toddlers are going through. Take a break from the insanity and read Jen's book. It's laugh-out-loud funny and jam-packed with parenting tips that really work!"
—Juli Auclair, host/Parents TV

"Just when you need it most, Jen Singer's books help remind you that laughter and a sense of humor are essential to parenting."
—Charlene Prince Birkeland, parenting editor for Yahoo! Shine and founder of crazedparent.org

"Smart, down-to-earth, hilarious, yet useful for real-life moms riding those everyday waves, Jen Singer's books are as essential as an extra diaper and that emergency cookie."

—Pamela Redmond Satran, coauthor of
Cool Names for Babies and *The Baby Name Bible*
and founder of nameberry.com

"Jen Singer offers up solid, field-tested parenting advice for weary moms. Her easy wit and humor deliver instant self-esteem and validation. She's the next best thing to having a sister or friend who's been through the tough early years of motherhood."

—Dr. Joshua Coleman, author of
When Parents Hurt and senior fellow with the
Council on Contemporary Families

"Everyone needs a mom-friend like Jen Singer. She shares the straight scoop on poopies, parties, and play dates, infusing motherhood with common sense, sanity, and sound advice. We can't all live next door to Jen (believe me, I wish I could), but you can still get the benefit of her wisdom and wit in her MommaSaid guides to motherhood. Being a mom is challenging enough. Jen makes it easier and more fun."

—Marybeth Hicks, columnist, *The Washington Times*;
author, *Bringing Up Geeks: How to Protect
Your Kid's Childhood in a Grow-Up-Too-Fast World*

STOP SECOND-GUESSING YOURSELF

Momma Said.net PRESENTS

YOURSELF

The Preschool Years

A Field-Tested Guide
to Confident Parenting

Jen Singer

Health Communications, Inc.
Deerfield Beach, Florida

www.hcibooks.com

Library of Congress Cataloging-in-Publication Data

Singer, Jen, 1967-
    Stop second-guessing yourself—the preschool years : the field-tested
guide to confident parenting / Jen Singer.
        p. cm.
    Includes index.
    ISBN-13: 978-0-7573-1417-9
    ISBN-10: 0-7573-1417-1
    1. Preschool children—Development.   2. Preschool children—Care.
3. Parent and child.   4. Parenting.   5. Child rearing.   I. Title.
HQ774.5.S558 2009
649'.122—dc22
                                                            2009012228

©2009 Jen Singer

Publisher: Health Communications, Inc.
        3201 S.W. 15th Street
        Deerfield Beach, FL 33442–8190

Cover design by Justin Rotkowitz
Interior design and formatting by Lawna Patterson Oldfield

For my father,
a.k.a. "Captain Red Pen"

Contents

Acknowledgments

Thanks to Allison Janse, editor and visionary, who e-mailed me one day and said, "How'd you like to write some books based on MommaSaid.net?" Your clever insight, superb editing, and unwavering loyalty when, in the middle of the whole thing, I got cancer, will be forever appreciated. Thanks to everyone at HCI for making this book series possible.

Thanks to Wendy Sherman and Ed Albowicz for your hard work, guidance, and friendship. Thanks to Robin Blakely for turning out magic, and for your continued support and love. Thanks, too, to Jenna Schnuer and Mark Stroginis for your work behind the scenes.

Thanks to my family: my mom and dad, my brother, Scott, all of my in-laws, my nieces, and my nephew.

Thanks to my husband, Pete, for continuing to be my biggest cheerleader and my best friend. And to our kids, Nicholas and Christopher, who fill my days with joy and laundry.

Thanks to my doctors, Julian Decter and Alison Grann, who helped return me to health (and hair).

Finally, thanks to MommaSaid's bloggers and our community of parents who help make it a fun place to visit and so graciously shared many fantastic tips and thoughts throughout this book.

Introduction

I guess I was a little too smug as I wandered around the super-market, humming to myself, thrilled that my four-year-old was staying at his preschool's aftercare program for the very first time. No more zooming around town like the Tasmanian Devil, racing from store to store, trying to get my errands done in the paltry two-and-a-half hours I had while he was in school. Thanks to aftercare, I could slow down a bit, taking my sweet time to put item after item onto the cashier's conveyor belt as I sipped my coffee and scanned magazine covers for celebrity gossip.

And then my cell phone rang.

"Mrs. Singer!" My son's teacher sounded annoyed. "Nicholas is very upset. He doesn't want to stay in aftercare. Come get him," she demanded.

"Can I buy a cantaloupe first?" I mumbled, but she'd already hung up. I frantically bagged my groceries and left for the pre-school.

Nicholas never stayed for aftercare again.

Two years later, I stayed home to sit by the phone when my son Christopher started aftercare at the preschool two days a week. I waited . . . and waited . . . and waited. But his teacher never called me. When I picked him up, he asked, "How come I can't go to aftercare every day?" And so, he did. And I finally got the chance to take my time at the supermarket and a whole lot more.

Welcome to the Preschool Years

While my kids' toddler years were a big blur of potty training, childproofing, and stuff lugging, their preschool years were something entirely different—something calmer, yes, but still surprising and, frankly, more fun. My boys had transitioned from barely verbal, bustling bundles of "Put that down!" to more articulate, somewhat rational smaller versions of grown-ups. It was like switching from Red Bull to decaf, or heavy metal to easy listening. Well, maybe not that smooth, but the years when my kids were ages three to five were a lot easier on me than their toddler years had been. If nothing else, I could finally shop in peace.

Less Likely to Dart into Traffic

Maybe you've noticed a change in your child, too. While your toddler was quick to dash off, laughing maniacally at you and your big ole pregnant belly while you shouted, "Get back here!" your preschooler at least thinks twice first before bolting. Or maybe she actually listens to you and even follows your instructions. Lucky you!

Maybe you're finally breathing a little easier—or maybe not. My older son skipped the terrible twos, instead opting for the tyrannical threes. I'm not even going to tell you what I called the fours. This is a family show.

See, while my preschoolers were a little less physically exhausting, they were sometimes more mentally draining. That's what happens when you add a dose of reasoning and longer term memory to the ability to protest. Preschoolers, it seems to me, are like little lawyers living in the house. "But Mom, you saaaaaid...." They sure are great at presenting their cases, aren't they?

But the preschool years are also a bit more nebulous, as your parenting concerns are no longer as concrete as, say, teaching the kids to walk or keeping them from climbing under the clothing racks at Sears. Now you've got tougher decisions (i.e., Montessori school or learn-through-play programs) and tougher questions (i.e., "Should I go back to work?" and "Why are tires black, Mommy?").

What MommaSaid About Preschoolers

When I launched MommaSaid.net, my website for beleaguered moms who could really use a laugh, I was right in the middle of the preschool years and all its construction paper crafts and stomach virus sharing. I was relieved to discover that other mothers were finding parts of parenting preschoolers to be as difficult as I had found high school chemistry class to be.

Through the years, the MommaSaid community has generously shared war stories, tips, advice and commiseration when it comes to parenting preschoolers—three- to five-year-old children who act a lot like tiny teens in light-up sneakers—increasingly independent and yet in dire need of your supervision and guidance, as they spend less and less time with you.

In this book, I've put together just about everything you need to know about raising preschoolers from my own experience as the mother of two former preschoolers, as well as from the veteran moms at MommaSaid.net, who've been in the trenches and have handled everything from that aching feeling you get at preschool drop-off to your three-year-old's newest addition to his arsenal: back talk.

It's the kind of back fence advice for surviving the preschool years you've wished you had ever since your kid went from tantruming toddler to negotiating preschooler. And it's what you'll reach for when you find yourself frantically bagging your cantaloupe, so you can get to preschool pick-up on time.

Throughout this guide, you'll find helpful quotes and tips from MommaSaid's moms and been-there, done-that stories and advice from this survivor of preschoolers, two times over. Most of all, you'll find help and validation in one easy-to-read book that you can keep bedside for night reading (now that you no longer doze off the moment your head hits the pillow) or whenever you've got some time when you aren't wondering why your preschooler and her playdate (and the markers they just disappeared with) have gotten way too quiet.

Remember, Momma said there'd be days like this. MommaSaid.net's: *Stop Second-Guessing Yourself—The Preschool Years* will help you not only endure them, but enjoy them, too.

WE ASKED: How is life with a preschooler different from life with a toddler?

"Easier in some ways, harder in others."

—*Lucinda, London, New Jersey*

"There are no diapers to change, no one waking up in the middle of the night, and no one trying to run into the street or sticking their hands in the toilet. But, emotionally, I find it harder. The discipline issues are more complicated, and the politics of preschool friendships are very complicated!"

—*Shoshana, Chicago, Illinois*

Just a minute!

Life with Preschoolers: The Game

START: First day of preschool

Your preschooler dashes into the classroom without any water works display. Quick! Run to your car! Move ahead three spaces.	Time Out.		No, your preschooler didn't just say "spit," but it rhymed with that. Go back to Time Out.			
			You find a drawing of yourself that says "I love Mommy" at Back-to-School Night. Move ahead to Hugs and Kisses.		Your preschooler's playdate brings homemade cookies! And strep throat. Move back one space.	
						Kids who didn't RSVP to your preschooler's birthday party show up—with their siblings. Move back two spaces.
			Preschooler makes you a Froot Loop necklace for Mother's Day. Move ahead to Hugs and Kisses.		Preschooler redecorates room with Sharpies and an attitude. Go back to Time Out.	Picky preschooler takes a liking to veggies. Go directly to next Hugs and Kisses.
						Time Out.

Your preschooler tells your neighbor you said he's a "big fat swob." Go back to Time Out.

Hugs and Kisses.

Your preschooler loses last pair of mittens—and it's only January. Lose a turn.

Your preschooler *finally* gives up her nighttime diaper. Move ahead to Hugs and Kisses.

Hugs and Kisses

Your preschooler presents arguments with the finesse of a seasoned defense attorney. Move back two spaces.

Your preschooler gives her little brother an extreme makeover. Take away the scissors and go back to Time Out.

Hugs and Kisses.

Your preschooler keeps her dress down on stage at graduation. Go to finish.

FINISH: Kindergarten.

Chapter One

So Long, Toddler:
Hello, Little Person with
Superb Negotiation Skills

WE ASKED: How are preschoolers different from toddlers?

"Compared to toddlers, preschoolers are more independent,
more talkative, less excitable, but more flexible.
Also more dramatic."

—*Michelle, Azusa, California*

My son Nicholas became a preschooler before he was in preschool. Not just because he turned three several months before starting preschool, but also because he started to stump Mommy. Suddenly, he wanted to know how things worked and why things were the way they were. And he expected me to know the answers.

"Are there potties in heaven?" he asked.

My answer: "Yes, and there are no lines for the ladies' room."

"What else is invisible besides air?" he questioned.

My answer: "Wonder Woman's airplane. And hydrogen."

"Do taxes hurt?" he wondered.

My answer: "Yes. Yes, they do."

While his little brother seemed more interested in such toddlerish activities as shoving as many toys into a tissue box as possible, it seemed that Nicholas had moved on, or perhaps up, to bigger kid concerns. And it became clear that the job of mothering him was about to change. Where I'd been physically challenged by two toddlers fueled by Goldfish crackers and pure boy energy, I was now going to be mentally challenged, too.

A friend told me, "Bigger kids, bigger problems," but I'm not sure if that's entirely true. I never had to scoop my preschoolers out of the tub before the water they'd turned on got hot. But my toddlers? Yes, indeed.

In fact, I found the preschool years to be much easier overall. Well, except for the year my older son was four. I'll go into it in detail in Chapter 5, where I'll talk about disciplining a child who would melt into the ground like the Wicked Witch of the West rather than accept "no" for an answer. But generally speaking, my preschoolers slept more and ran off less as they moved away from their toddler years and toward what I like to call the age of reason.

I'll touch on some of the main differences between toddlers and preschoolers here to prime you for the how-to part of the rest of the book. Perhaps you've already seen the changes I'm talking about. Or maybe you're too busy trying to figure out if there are potties in heaven to notice.

WE ASKED: Are/were the preschool years harder or easier than the toddler years?

Easier: 52%
Harder: 32%
Not sure: 15%

#1: Preschoolers Go to School

AS MY NOW tweens would say: Duh. Except, sending your baby off to school is perhaps the most exciting, wonderful, . . . traumatic, frightening, and harrowing part of your child's preschool years. You will likely spend oodles of time trying to find the right school with the right program for your kid, and you'll encounter all sorts of issues you hadn't experienced when you had a toddler in your care.

You might have to decide whether your preschooler is ready for drop-off playdates, kiddie sports, and video games. You might feel the pressure to finish up potty training before school starts, or to teach your child the ABCs, 123s, and more.

If your toddler wasn't in day care, you'll be faced with exposing

Okay, I admit it. . . .

"They just seem to be so grown up at times. They also seem to see the world outside of their own little worlds."

—*Sachia, Independence, Missouri*

your preschooler to other kids (and their germs and bad words, among other things). You might be starting homeschooling or karate or any other number of activities that weren't a part of your toddler's life. In other words, the school years change everything. Are you ready?

#2: Preschoolers Reach More Nebulous Milestones

WHILE YOUR TODDLER learned the grand slams of milestones—walking, talking, potty training—the milestones your three- to five-year-old will reach are a little less concrete. (Unless, of course, you're still trying to potty train. But I'll go over that in Chapter 3).

You'll soon become well versed in fine versus gross motor skills, cognitive issues, socialization, and kindergarten readiness. Sometimes you'll be called upon to help your preschooler meet these milestones. Other times, they're better off left alone.

Okay, I admit it. . . .

"It was easier to take a toddler to where you want to go and what you want to do as opposed to my preschooler, who's already trying to go and do what she wants."

—*Maria, Arlington, Texas*

Wading your way through these complex milestones can be difficult, if not confounding at times. But you've likely got the benefit of a preschool teacher and a pediatrician to help guide you through. And you've got the tips and advice from this book to help prepare you.

#3: Preschoolers Have an Expanding Social Calendar and More Activities

UNTIL MY KIDS were in preschool, I pretty much had ultimate control over their social calendars. I chose who they'd play with and when. But in preschool, they made friends, and these friends wanted to come to my house, even if I'd planned an afternoon of cleaning out the closets while my kids did their own thing in their rooms.

Soon, I was driving a car full of children to kiddie soccer and picking up a son or two from various neighbors' homes. The "mom calendar" my aunt had given me suddenly made sense. When my kids were toddlers, I had no need for a calendar with columns for each family member's activities. By preschool, however, I needed it, because I had to keep track of not just my time, but also my kids' activities, which didn't always include me.

I started to put more miles on my car (and cleaned out more crumbs and dirt), and I got out of the house

Okay, I admit it. . . .

"Each age is equally frustrating, but with my toddler, I seem to not get as mad because in my mind he is still a baby, whereas my preschooler cries to get attention, even if it is negative. The difference is he knows what he is doing."

—*Anjanette, Springfield, Illinois*

Okay, I admit it. . . .

"They're learning all sorts of lovely (note the sarcasm) words and attitudes from other kids in preschool, and bringing them home!"

—*Stephanie, St. Paul, Minnesota*

Okay, I admit it. . . .

"If you skipped the Terrible Twos, don't get excited; it will come when they are three."

—*Melanie, Booneville, Arkansas*

just about every day. Thanks to my preschoolers, I became busier and busier. In time, I learned how to best manage it all. I'll share my tips later on.

#4: Disciplining Preschoolers Is a Bit More Complicated

REMEMBER HOW CONCERNED you were about your toddler learning how to talk? Well, now you might wonder why you worried at all. Your preschooler not only can talk, but he can negotiate like a lawyer in mediation. If you don't learn how to discipline a preschooler, you might find yourself defending your decisions and rules all day long. I know. I've been there.

When my older son was four, the magic of time-outs started to wear off, and suddenly, I had to figure out how to get my son to do what I wanted him to do without ending up arguing over everything and then giving up entirely.

Okay, I admit it. . . .

"They act like teenagers. One day they are pleasant; the next day they aren't. You walk around on egg shells because you never know what is going to set them off."

—*Kristina, Marysville, Ohio*

If you find that disciplining your preschooler is far more complicated than it was during the toddler years, you're not alone. Later, I'll provide some secrets for keeping the peace at home and out and about.

#5: Your Preschooler Deals with Family Members Differently

WHEN MY OLDER son started his second year of preschool, he lost some Omi time. Until then, he'd spent just about every Thursday with my mother-in-law, whom we call "Omi," while I went out to run errands, get a haircut, or drive around talking to myself. Sud-

> **Okay, I admit it. . . .**
>
> "Sometimes their attitude can push you to the edge. I always thought that would come later in his life."
>
> —*Leah, Phoenix, Arizona*

denly, he had to share his Thursdays with his preschool teacher, and my mother-in-law lost some of her routine time with him. They still adored each other, but it was clear that things weren't the same.

It isn't just school that can affect your preschooler's relationships. It's also your preschooler. She's older, a little more mature, and a lot more talkative. She's more opinionated and has her own ideas on how to spend her time—and who to spend it with.

Whether there's a new baby in your house or your preschooler thinks she's now old enough to hang out with her older siblings, things have changed. I'll cover not only what can change, but how to manage it.

> **Okay, I admit it. . . .**
>
> "Age three was very teary. Not tantrumy, just dramatic sobbing—or could that have been because of the arrival of a little sister?"
>
> —*Michelle, Azusa, California*

#6: Your Preschooler Can Entertain Himself Now . . . Sorta

Okay, I admit it. . . .

"They are still small enough to love unconditionally, and not afraid to show it, yet old enough that it means something beyond 'I appreciate whoever gives me milk.'"

—*Aubrey, Allegan, Michigan*

TAKING A TODDLER to the movies is like bringing a puppy to church. Nobody's going to sit down for long, and you'll be shushing a lot. But preschoolers? That's something different. Not completely though—preschoolers are still all too likely to stage-whisper midfilm, "Mommy? Why is that lion wearing pants?"

But entertaining a preschooler is easier than wrangling a toddler. At least you're not pulling the refrigerator magnets off the fridge and putting them back on again . . . and again . . . and again.

The most important part of entertaining your preschooler is to teach him to entertain himself. It'll be good for him as he learns to be more independent. And it'll

Okay, I admit it. . . .

"My son is five and is deep into his Star Wars phase. Every conversation is about Star Wars. He would watch Star Wars movies all day long if I would let him."

—*Jamie, Hudson, Wisconsin*

be good for you as you try to get something done around the house for once. I'll offer up the best ways to entertain your preschooler, from toys to games to activities, as well as ways to teach him to keep himself busy while you do something else altogether.

#7: Your Preschooler Will Have a Whole Lotta Questions

BE PREPARED FOR the number one question you'll get the next few years: "Why?" Your preschooler will want to know why things are the way they are, from why grass is green to why Daddy gets to put his feet on the couch when you just told your preschooler to get hers off. Why, why, why? If you don't know why, it can be either fun or exhausting finding the answer. And if you do know why, but really don't want to take the time to explain to your preschooler, say, why you get to have a cookie before dinner but your preschooler doesn't—it can be tiring.

Preschoolers are naturally inquisitive. At times, it'll be fun to see the world through their eyes. Other times, it'll be aggravating to be interrogated when you just want to listen to the radio while you drive home. I'll cover the why behind your preschooler's whys

Okay, I admit it. . . .

"As toddlers, they couldn't communicate as well, but now as preschoolers everything is 'But, why, Mommy?' And they think they know everything about everything."

—*Helene, Stockton, California*

Okay, I admit it. . . .

"As you're rushing to the PTA meeting after the Daisy meeting after soccer practice after grocery shopping after work, it's hard to find even the few minutes to remind your child of proper behavior. We're often so harried that we don't do so in a productive way and instead make them feel awful by yelling. It's ugly to do to the child and ugly for other people who are around."

—*Kristin, Chesapeake, Virginia*

Okay, I admit it. . . .

"It's much easier to sit them in front of a television or computer game than to take time to teach or discipline a child in the correct way to behave."

—*Debra, Harlingen, Texas*

and how to handle these most inquisitive of your children's years.

#8: You'll Need to Teach Your Preschooler Manners

REPEAT AFTER ME: "What do you say?" No, don't repeat it. You're probably already saying it a hundred times a day as you try to teach your child to say "please," "thank you" and "I'm sorry." Yet now that you've got a preschooler, you should step it up a notch, teaching her everything from proper table manners to caring for the less fortunate. Only, that's hard to do when your preschooler still believes the entire world revolves around her.

Okay, I admit it. . . .

"It goes fast, which sounds like so much B.S. to anyone who hasn't been through it, but I can't believe my five-year-old has just four more months to go until she's done with pre-school!"

—*Adam, Allendale, New Jersey*

If you wait too long to instill manners in your child, however, it might end up being too late. Luckily, preschoolers still like to please Mommy, and they like to act all grown-up. I'll show you how to use this to your advantage as you go about teaching your preschooler how to behave when you're not there to remind her, "What do you say?"

#9: Preschoolers Have to Get Ready for Kindergarten

THERE AS A TIME when all a kid had to do to get ready for kindergarten was turn five. But things have changed. Certainly, preschool goes a long way to prepare your kid for the increasingly academic kindergarten classes of today. If you're lucky, that's all your preschooler will need to be prepared. But sometimes there's more to consider, including your preschooler's maturity, fine motor skills, and patience—or lack thereof.

I'm not suggesting you hold up flash cards for your preschooler while you sit at stop lights. Nor am I trying to scare you. But the reality of kindergarten in the twenty-first century is something more complex than you grew up with way back when. I'll explain what today's kindergarten teachers are looking for and what you can do to get your preschooler ready for next year.

Okay, I admit it. . . .

"I think this stage is quicker than we realize. Once they start school, the end is beginning!"

—*Chrissy, Dillsburg, Pennsylvania*

Okay, I admit it. . . .

"He is learning so fast; we can't keep up with him."

—*Kristina, Marysville, Ohio*

#10: Preschoolers Are More Independent— and That Might Bother You

PERSONALLY, I COULDN'T wait for my kids to not need me quite so much. And yet, it took me a while to figure out how to make them more independent. I guess it's because I felt it was my job to be there for them 24/7. Also, if they didn't need me quite so much, what was I supposed to do? Read the newspaper? Oh, that would have been fabulous! Why didn't I think of that?

Today's moms are faced with safety issues that our mothers never had to deal with. Plus, we've been charged with maximizing our children's "teachable moments" while preparing them for a much more intense school experience than we had to handle. So it's no wonder we're a bit, shall we say, protective.

But when we take our care and concern a little too far, our preschoolers suffer because they don't learn how to be independent. And you can't be at school to zipper your preschooler's coat before playtime. I'll explain how you can teach your preschooler to be more independent—and how to be okay with it. Really.

Okay, I admit it. . . .

"I used to visit the school to see if she was behaving right and also checking on the teachers."

—*Sherry, Paterson, New Jersey*

Okay, I admit it. . . .

"I shopped at Target with my younger son during preschool hours. We saved no money during that time."

—*Kristina, Marysville, Ohio*

#11: Preschool Is a Great Time to Get More Time for Yourself

I STARTED MOMMASAID.NET when my younger son was in preschool. It was time for me to realize what Mr. Rogers had once sung on TV while I sobbed quietly with my two toddlers in my lap: "You are more than any one part of you." In other words, I was more than a mom. And it was time to put the "me" back in "mommy" for a change.

Though, I admit that I grappled with guilt for even thinking of starting my own business. I felt it was a privilege to stay home with my kids, and so, I ought to do it all the time. But when my website started to take off, I realized it was okay for me to want something that's my own. And now, years later, I know my kids think so, too. Whether you're planning to start a business, volunteer, go back to work, or take up an activity that has nothing to do with motherhood, the preschool years can be a great time to start. I'll cover what you can do with your time—and how to get that time.

Okay, I admit it. . . .

"I felt I still needed to keep my eyes on my toddlers all the time. Not so with a preschooler."

—*Jen, Fort Thomas, Kentucky*

Okay, I admit it. . . .

"When I have a conference call, I just pray my mute button works on my phone."

—*Barbara, Arlington, Virginia*

#12: Your Own Situation Will Affect How You Parent Your Preschooler

NOT JUST YOUR preschooler, but all of your kids. Whether you're divorced, parenting while ill, working from home, or waiting for your spouse to return from his tour of duty, your particular situation comes into play when you're parenting. And that's okay.

Don't think you're the first mother to plop in a video for the kids so you can take a conference call, call your lawyer, e-mail your military spouse, or put your feet up after chemotherapy. MommaSaid's fans and I will offer up our top tips for handling the situation, whatever yours may be.

Okay, I admit it. . . .

"Life with a preschooler is so much different because now they have opinions and voice those opinions, whether it's about what to eat, what to wear, or anything else that they want control over. You learn to pick your battles!"

—*Stacey, Anaheim, California*

Okay, I admit it. . . .

"It has been more fun, yet frustrating at the same time!"

—*Danelle, Middleburg Heights, Ohio*

Gimme a break

Curb your Baby Lust.

If you've got baby lust, don't let your preschooler know it. Whether you're planning to have another baby or not, it isn't fair to your preschooler to tell him you miss having a baby around the house. That would be like your husband telling you he misses being married to someone ten years younger. So be discreet when you go around breathing in baby powder and longing for the pitter patter of feet littler than your preschooler has. It's only fair to him.

"⏰" Just a minute!

Toddler or Preschooler?
Here's How to Tell the Difference

Toddler	Preschooler
Shows disinterest in the activity you have chosen by dashing off in the opposite direction.	Shows disinterest in the activity you have chosen by ticking off reasons you have, once again, failed to meet her entertainment needs.
Refuses to potty train by hiding behind the toy box and going in his Pull-Ups.	Refuses to potty train by hiding behind the toy box, going on the floor, and then blaming the dog.
Runs to greet you enthusiastically, as though you had been missing at sea and presumed dead.	Runs to greet you enthusiastically, as though you had been missing at sea along with the doll you had promised to bring back for her.
Engages in "parallel play."	Engages in "cooperative play," even though you have no desire to be a fire engine driver for the next hour or so.
Mumbles to herself, though you don't understand what she's saying.	Mumbles to herself, though you don't understand where she picked up *that* word.

Chapter Two

Out There on Her Own
Your Baby's Off to Preschool
(at Some Point)

 WE ASKED: What criteria did you use to choose a preschool for your child?

"For my oldest daughter, a teacher who wouldn't scare her. For my youngest, a teacher who had the experience to be wise to her tricks and love her anyway."

—*Jennifer, Puyallup, Washington*

The moment I spotted the glass jars, I knew this wasn't the place for my son. I had brought my three-year-old to a local Montessori school during my first (and last) extensive Tour de Preschools to find the right school for my son to spend his mornings. But when the director showed me a preschooler-level cubby filled with breakable items designed to "teach our students responsibility," I knew my rambunctious son wouldn't fit in there. Rather, he'd be more interested in studying cause and effect while standing over the broken glass on the floor.

But I nodded and smiled, as if to say, "Well, of course my child knows how to care for fine breakables." And then whenever I spotted the school's director in the supermarket, I ducked into the frozen veggies aisle to hide.

In the end, I chose our church's preschool program, because its learn-through-play format suited my son's needs. Also, they kept glass out of reach, just like I did.

In short, it just seemed like we were on the same page.

When it was my younger son's turn to start preschool, I already knew where he'd attend. The church program had done right by his big brother, and so I signed him up there, too, thereby ensuring the safety of the Montessori's glass jars from yet another Singer boy.

Okay, I admit it. . . .

"We're not the norm when it comes to selecting schools. We had just moved to the area and needed to make friends. I chose the school because it would accept my two-year-old. And it worked. We've made some great friends!"

—*Chrissy, Dillsburg, Pennsylvania*

Planning for Preschool

WHILE THREE- TO five-year-olds clearly still need momma in a big way, preschool is their first real shot at all sorts of milestones. They form their own friendships and, sometimes, their own style.

(When else can you wear a Disney Princess gown in April?) What's more, their personalities really start to blossom and, at times, explode. Once they get through the separation anxiety, Mom can start to reclaim bits of time for herself. *Two-and-a-quarter hours just for me! Work out? Shop? Nap? What to do? What to do!*

But just because your child is three, doesn't mean she's necessarily ready for preschool. Maybe she's simply not suited for the preschool you had your heart set on. Or maybe you want to skip preschool altogether and keep her home.

Here, I'll offer up questions to ask and things to keep in mind when searching for a preschool, and how to figure out if your child is even ready for school in the first place. Meanwhile, go get that Disney Princess gown ready, just in case.

Your Kid's Birthday Isn't Necessarily a Sign of Preschool Readiness

JUST BECAUSE ALL the other three-year-olds in the neighborhood are starting preschool in the fall doesn't necessarily mean you should start stocking up on the graham crackers and juice for preschool snack time just yet. How can you be sure your child is ready for preschool? Consider these guidelines:

1. **Is she old enough?** Many preschools set age limits on their classes, which are often tied to the town's public school enrollment cutoffs. If your child has a late birthday, meaning it's close to the elementary school's cutoff date, you

might end up delaying kindergarten a year. Ask yourself if you want her to have an extra year of preschool or an extra year at home before she even starts preschool.

2. **Is your child fairly independent?** There are basic tasks your child should be able to do before entering preschool, including washing hands, eating without assistance (a sandwich, not a porterhouse steak), and putting on a jacket. If your child can't do these tasks, take a look at how much you help him in a day. If you rush in to help too quickly, he won't learn to be independent in time for preschool to start. Back off, and let him learn some of the basics of self-care, so he can get ready for school.

3. **Is she potty trained?** Not all preschools require your child to be potty trained, but many do. If your child isn't in underpants yet, with accidents few and far between, you might want to rethink preschool for now. Or you might want to hunker down and finish up potty training. See Chapter 3 for details on how to potty train late bloomers (and stubborn poopers).

4. **Have you two been apart much?** If you and your preschooler have been as inseparable as the dog and his favorite chewy toy, it's going to be harder to get your child to saunter into preschool with nary a wistful glance your way. Start preparing your little one for time away from you by leaving him with a family member or trusted babysitter for periods of time. Once he learns that Mommy always

comes back, it'll be easy for him to separate from you at preschool.

5. **Do you keep a schedule?** Preschool is very orderly. Children are expected to follow the classroom's daily plan—from circle time to the daily book reading to arts and crafts—your child will be expected to move from activity to activity. If your child is used to a looser schedule, she might refuse to stop playing with the dollhouse and work on her ABCs like everyone else. Start sticking to a schedule for a few months before school starts to help her get used to structured time.

6. **Does she like to play in groups?** A kid who loves circle time at Mommy & Me class will be more likely to jump right into the classroom's group activities at preschool. But your child doesn't have to be the mayor of Socialville to be ready for school. Help get her accustomed to groups by taking her to organized activities, such as story time at the library or a kiddie gymnastic program.

7. **Can he follow instructions?** By the time your child is three, he should be able to follow simple one- or two-step instructions. He doesn't have to jump up enthusiastically every time you tell him to do something, but he needs to be able to, say, open the door for the cat or put his sippy cup in the sink if you ask him to. Just imagine what it's like to get twenty three-year-olds to line up to go outside, and you'll understand why this is so important for preschoolers.

8. **Does she nap?** If your child still takes an afternoon nap, you may want to consider a preschool that meets in the morning. You don't want your child to end up exhausted and cranky toward the end of each school day.

9. **Does your child have special needs?** If your child has developmental or language delays or physical disabilities, you may need extra time to find the right preschool program for him. Ask your pediatrician, occupational or physical therapist, or other parents of children with similar issues for the best programs in your area.

10. **Are *you* ready for preschool?** Before you fill out the enrollment form, ask yourself why you want your child to start preschool. Is it because you think he's ready for social interaction and far more clever crafts than you can muster up? Or is it because your mother made you feel guilty for keeping him home? Make sure you're signing up for preschool for the right reasons before you rush in.

"The socialization garnered from being in school makes a world of difference in a preschooler's temperament."

It worked for me!

—*Sarah, Northbridge, Massachusetts*

WE ASKED: What's the best part about parenting a preschooler?

"Just last month, I had my hair cut without simultaneously entertaining a child for the first time in eight years."

—Jennifer, Puyallup, Washington

What Kind of Preschool Is Right for Your Kid?

WHEN I WAS four, I attended a preschool that involved a couple of hours of playing and a brief nap time when we were supposed to lie on mats and rest. But really, Paula Patterson and I spent it making funny faces at each other.

Today, there are many different options when it comes to the type of preschool your child can attend. It's up to you to decide which one works best for your family.

First, you have to determine if you want your child to attend day care or a preschool. The difference is that day care often offers longer hours and less academic pursuits. A preschool traditionally involves a few hours a day of instruction, though some, such as Montessori, often provide full-day preschool classes.

Next, you have to decide what kind of teaching philosophy you're looking for in a preschool. Here are some of the most common types:

Academic

The philosophy: Preschoolers need to prepare for the upper grades where academics are king. In fact, academic preschools feel more like kindergartens with their structured, curriculum-based learning. They generally aren't all books and rote teaching, though; kids at these preschools do get to play. But academic preschools expect their students to follow a set program as a class, just like the bigger kids do, and they emphasize book learning more than, say, researching the minute-by-minute actions of the class guinea pig.

For which kids? If you've got a fidgety kid who'd rather study her Dora light-up sneakers than her shapes, this likely isn't the right program for her. But if you've got a good listener and avid learner, an academic preschool might be the place she'll blossom.

Cooperative

The philosophy: It's all about the group, not really the individual. Cooperative preschools require regular parent involvement in the classroom and at meetings. They tend to offer play-based curricula in a social atmosphere, creating a family feel your child might not find at a larger school.

For which kids? Or more appropriately, which parents? If you're working full time or if you have other kids at home, you might find it difficult to meet the parent volunteer requirements of a co-op preschool. But if you have one child and/or enough time, this could be the right program for your family.

Learn Through Play

The philosophy: Kids learn best through play. Play-centered preschools tend to focus on play-based learning with less of an emphasis on academics. For example, kids learn how things work by knocking over their block tower or by squooshing Play-Doh. They also learn their ABCs and other preschool-level academic lessons, but you probably won't find kids sitting at desks while teachers lecture at learn-through-play preschools.

For which kids? If you've got a so-called high energy child, this is probably the place for him. Here, he'll be able to play for a few hours with minimal structured group activities, which tend to be fun (and sometimes, loud).

Okay, I admit it. . . .

"Go with your gut! Stop in unannounced and trust how you feel and what you feel from the teachers and the kids who are attending."

—*Jen, Fort Thomas, Kentucky*

Montessori

The philosophy: Developed in Italy by Maria Montessori, the country's first female physician, this program is based on the belief that children will teach themselves if you give them the right environment. Classes are arranged by varying age groups, so your three-year-old might be in the same class as some six-year-olds who, presumably, will help teach the younger kids. Group activities aren't a big part of most Montessori schools, where children are expected to be self-directed. Note that toys aren't a part of the Montessori program, which might seem odd to parents who aren't familiar with the Montessori approach.

For which kids? If your child prefers to learn at his or her own pace, rather than keeping up with the class, perhaps a Montessori school would work well for her. Independent kids with self-control fit well here. Think of the three-year-old who likes to study how caterpillars crawl or will sit and read to himself for extended periods of time. Plus, Montessori schools often extend their offerings beyond the typical few morning hours and through grade school, so, if you can afford it, you can give your kids the Montessori style of learning into the elementary school years.

Religion Based

The philosophy: Introducing children to religious education at young ages helps foster their faith in God. Most religion-based preschools offer play-centered programs that mix basic religious principles into their curricula. In addition to all the usual preschool-level lessons at play-centered programs, kids learn prayers and discuss God in an age-appropriate way.

For which kids? If you plan to enroll your child in a religious kindergarten and elementary school, a religion-based preschool will give him a head start. But religion-based preschools aren't just for the religious. Some parents see it as a basic introduction to religion, while others just like the school's overall program. In fact, you don't necessarily have to belong to the same religion for your child to attend. Ask the school's administrators for details.

Reggio Emilia

The philosophy: Named after the city in Italy where Loris Malaguzzi founded the first preschool of its kind, this approach to learning gives the child more power than in traditional authority-based preschools. Big on arts and hands-on activities, this program is based on the idea that teachers encourage, rather than teach, and that parents are partners in learning. In other words, this isn't your typical preschool.

For which kids? If your child is creative and social, Reggio Emilia might work well for her. But if you've got a kid who likes to play alone or hates arts and crafts, you might want to consider another program.

Waldorf

The philosophy: Created by Austrian philosopher Dr. Rudolf Steiner, Waldorf schools are all about building children's imaginations in a noncompetitive atmosphere that eschews modern media. As a result, it tends to attract the Birkenstock crowd who like the schools' all-natural approach: nothing in the classroom is made from plastic or other nonorganic materials. Kids stay with one teacher (who may not be state certified, but is likely certified by Waldorf Schools of North America) from preschool through eighth grade. Academics aren't necessarily the priority.

For which kids? If you embrace or don't mind the school's basis in anthroposophy, Steiner's belief that human intellect holds the ability to contact spiritual worlds, Waldorf might well suit your creative child who has minimal interest in academics.

> **It worked for me!**
>
> "My oldest son turned five in August, and we decided to hold off on kindergarten until he was six. So we wanted a preschool that was five days a week. There were only two in our city. We chose the newer, brighter looking preschool. It turned out to be a wonderful preschool."
>
> —Anjanette, Springfield, Illinois

WE ASKED: What were your biggest concerns about preschool?

My child would have a hard time leaving me: 56%
I would have a hard time leaving my child: 37%
My child wouldn't make friends or get along with the other kids: 37%
My preschooler would get sick often: 30%
My child wouldn't be able to use the toilet on his/her own: 16%
The school day was too long: 12%
My child would prefer school to being with me: 5%
The school day was too short: 5%

Are You Cut Out for Homeschooling?

FOR SOME PARENTS, homeschooling is a way of life. For others, it's a way to save money on preschool. If you decide that homeschooling is the right thing for your preschooler, consider, too, whether it's right for you. Before you research how to homeschool your preschooler, ask yourself:

Am I ready to face the criticism? The majority of parents send their three- and four-year-olds to preschool. Prepare yourself for criticism at the playground and at birthday parties.

Do I have the time? Homeschooling preschoolers doesn't take as much time as it does for older kids, but you still need to carve out the time. If you're working or have other children, you need to find the time to homeschool your little one.

Can I afford it? Factor in your lost income if you choose to stay home and homeschool.

Do I have the temperament? Homeschooling is more involved than stay-at-home motherhood. Sneaking in a lesson about colors in the produce aisle isn't the kind of commitment that homeschooling requires. Plus, it requires you to be with your child a lot more than usual. If you're the type who needs alone time, think about the time constraints. Make sure you're cut out to teach your preschooler before you jump in.

Are you good at setting up a social calendar? You'll need to make sure your preschooler has a chance to socialize with other kids. If all the neighborhood kids are in day care all day, or if you're too shy to reach out to other parents, you'll have difficulty getting your child involved with other kids.

Okay, I admit it. . . .

"His first year of preschool was pretty rough; he clung to my leg and had a hard time separating . . . there were lots of tantrums, and so on. His second year went very well on the whole, and he ran into the room willingly, usually without even giving me a hug or a kiss."

—*Stephanie, St. Paul, Minnesota*

Gimme a break

Start Planning for Preschool Early

Don't wait until a week before preschool registration to start thinking about a school for your child, or you'll end up in a mad school-to-school dash like a contestant on *Supermarket Sweep*. A few months before preschool sign-ups, start interviewing parents with kids in preschool now and those with older kids. Go to each school's open house and ask questions of the teachers and administrators. When you've narrowed down your choices (assuming there are choices in your area), make an appointment to stop in and watch a class in action. You'll learn a lot about how the teachers handle all sorts of personalities and issues, and you'll get a taste of what your child's day would be like there.

Just a minute!

Are You Ready for Preschool, Mom?

A Mini Preschool Aptitude Test

Read the selections below and then choose the correct answers.

1. Your child has come home from preschool with knowledge of a new-to-her four-letter word, courtesy of one of her dear little class-mates. It's the same word you mumbled when this very same child passed along the stomach flu, first to your kid and then to everyone in the house except the dog, who drinks from the toilet and never throws up. When you hear the word come out of your sweet cherub's mouth, you:

   a. Gasp and start fanning yourself like a character on *The Stepford Wives.*

   b. Nonchalantly say it, too, as an adjective, adverb, and noun, thereby taking away its appeal and hopefully, its continued use.

   c. Promptly change preschools.

   d. Blog about it, changing the names to protect the not-so-innocent, hoping it'll embarrass that kid's mother into cleaning up her mouth.

   e. Report it to the teacher even though it makes you feel like a fourth grader to tattle, "Olivia used a bad word!"

2. You're standing in line at Target when you glance at your watch and realize that the preschool, located thirteen minutes away (if you hit all green lights), lets out in eleven minutes. You don't want to be late to pick up your child, but you also really, really need to buy pajamas, cereal, a mattress pad, four bars of soap, a pair of shorts for you, some allergy medicine, and a shower curtain adorned with very cute cartoon monkeys. (Okay, maybe not the shower curtain.) When the old lady in front of you asks

for a price check on a bra the size of hammock, you:

a. Ditch your cart and dash out the store while shouting to the clerk, "I've got an emergency!"

b. Assure her that it's $20 and hand her the cash for it, hoping it'll move her along more quickly.

c. Cut off another mom headed for the only free register and wildly throw your stuff on the conveyor belt while frantically dialing the class mom to pick up your child—again.

d. Vow to shop online until your child graduates from high school.

e. Quietly hide the cart in the men's department and come back for it after preschool pick-up—or perhaps, the next morning.

3. It's show and tell day, only you've just found that out with about four minutes until preschool starts. You root through your purse, and hand your child a quarter. "Here, tell them all about how George Washington is on the quarter," you say in your singsong mommy voice. But your child replies, "We're supposed to bring in something that begins with 'R.'" So you:

a. Hand him a receipt for two pregnancy tests and a urinary tract infection test kit and, for the first time all semester, thank God your child can't read yet.

b. Wonder why the hell America has no coins that begin with "R."

c. Hand him your blush, telling him Grandma calls it "rouge," while hoping he doesn't take a liking to it or any other makeup.

d. Marvel at the excellent selection your car's floor has to offer, including: a *Ratatouille* T-shirt in 3T, an empty *r*aspberry juice box, gummy *r*abbits from an Easter party, the baby's *r*ash ointment, and a box of Rice-A-Roni that had fallen out of your grocery bag.

Chapter Three

Still Not a Chatty Cathy or a Dapper Dan?
Milestones You Don't Have to Lose Sleep Over—and Those You Might

WE ASKED: How is life with a preschooler different from life with a toddler?

"You definitely start to feel pressure to potty train, to transition from a crib to a bed, and basically to start to ensure that your Terrible Two's toddler suddenly starts exhibiting human traits."

—Sarah, Northbridge, Massachusetts

When my older son was in preschool, his fine motor skills were so far behind the norm he pretty much scribbled his name and then promptly lost interest in drawing much of anything. His ability to make small muscle movements with his fingers hadn't yet caught up to where his teachers expected them to be in preschool.

While this may seem like it should be no big deal, in today's increasingly academic curricula for kindergartners, it meant my son would likely struggle in the grades ahead until his fine motor skills improved. Think about it: you need fine motor skills to be able to write, cut, trace, and color, not to mention zipper, button, and fasten. In other words, fine motor skills are the foundation of today's kindergarten.

When my son walked out of the preschool with his drawing of "you, Mommy!"—a blob of pink scribble—I was perfectly content . . . until I saw the other kids' drawings. Some of the girls' work was like Leonardo da Vinci's in comparison.

So his teacher recommended that I try to strengthen my son's fine motor skills by setting aside time to fiddle with Play-Doh, color, and draw using a special pencil attachment that made it easier for him to grip while writing.

Let me make this clear: I didn't drill him on his fine motor skills every day. He hated drawing and writing—and with good reason. He didn't have the control he needed to make it fun for him. Besides, an occupational therapist and his pediatrician told me that most kids will gain fine motor skills as they age. In other words, what he really needed was time. And we gave it to him by delaying kindergarten a year, in part because of his lagging fine motor skills, but also because he lacked the maturity for our kindergarten's intensely academic program.

Within a year, not only did his fine motor skills "kick in," but also he quickly became the class artist. Now a tween, he draws a four-page weekly comic strip in which local stores advertise. Kids even commission artwork from him, which they hang on refrigerator doors throughout town.

So did I really have to worry when he was in preschool? Looking back, probably not. His delayed fine motor skills didn't really need professional assistance or my diligent managing. Turns out, my own Leonardo da Vinci just needed time.

If your child is in preschool or about to start, you're going to have a lot of chances to compare her abilities to everyone else's. But when do you need to take action, and when should you just chill out and see how it goes? The answer lies in understanding which milestones matter the most and what's expected of your child in preschool. I'll cover the basics in this chapter.

WE ASKED: What was the worst part about having a preschooler?

"Knowing that I am responsible for the future. What I can, or can't teach this child today will affect him tomorrow."

—Jill, Toledo, Ohio

Getting Your Child Ready for Preschool

THOUGH YOU MAY be tempted to get your kid ready for preschool by quizzing her on everything from the colors of the apples in the produce aisle to the numbers on gasoline pumps, ease up a little on the teachable moments. Your child's preschool teacher probably wants her to be as socially prepared as possible, not necessarily academically proficient. So how can you help get her ready?

Teach him to put on his own coat. It sounds like it should be no big deal, but imagine you're a preschool teacher, and you've got twenty kids to get ready to go outside to play or head home, and none of them know how to put on a coat. By the time you help them all out, it'll be spring. Teach your child how to put on a coat before preschool starts, and you'll do the teacher—and your child—a favor.

Teach her how to share. It'll help cut down on preschool scuffles over toys, playground slides, and snacks.

Teach him how to use the potty. Some preschools require children to be able to use the toilet on their own. But even if your child's school doesn't, potty training is a rite of passage that most children complete by age three—around the time preschool usually starts.

Teach her how to sit still (or at least more still than usual). Before they started preschool, my boys weren't great sitters—not when there was so much to see in the toy box and under the couch and wherever the cat was. But they learned how to sit better simply by attending Playorama classes, where they were expected (though never forced) to sit for parts of the class. By the time they started school, they got the gist of circle time to sit while in class well enough.

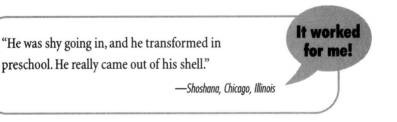

"He was shy going in, and he transformed in preschool. He really came out of his shell."

—*Shoshana, Chicago, Illinois*

It worked for me!

"My older son came out of his shell, and my younger son got the discipline of listening to a teacher and sitting for circle time."

It worked for me!

— Juliet, Albany, New York

What to Expect—For Real

I REMEMBER READING to my preschool class when I was only four. And yet, I was jealous of Suzanne Sullivan, who already knew how to tie her shoes when I didn't. Plus, she had these really cool red sneakers. Oh, how I wanted to have my own red sneakers and the so very grown-up ability to tie them. And though she didn't know how to read, and I couldn't tie my shoes, we both grew up just fine. Maybe that's because our parents didn't push us to learn things before our time. I wonder if that could happen today.

From the moment we get our baby's APGAR score at the hospital, we, as twenty-first-century parents, start comparing and measuring our kids against everyone else's, as though childhood is a competition filled with resume-building activities. Before preschool, your child has likely hit all of major developmental milestones, the ones baby books help you diligently mark, like talking and walking. In preschool, however, things get a little more nebulous. Does your preschooler need to be able to write his name or recite the alphabet? Does she have to be able to ride a bike or skip or jump? How much should he be talking?

Remember that every kid develops at her own pace. Still, there comes a time when your child's missed milestone can become an issue. Here are a few preschool-age milestones to consider, along with "get real" advice for when to worry, and when not to.

Gives up napping. The majority of kids give up naps by age three, but about ten percent hang on to their PM snooze until age five. (Hey, I still need one now and then.) My older son, God bless him, didn't give up his afternoon nap until he turned four.

Get real: As long as she's waking up from her nap in a good mood, and then falls asleep at a decent hour each night without a problem, while getting close to twelve hours of solid sleep a night, napping is probably okay at this stage. But check with your pediatrician if you think your preschooler seems unusually tired or listless.

Runs, jumps, and skips. Most kids can run, climb, skip, jump in place, ride a tricycle, kick a ball, and walk up and down stairs using alternate feet by age three.

Get real: Remember, I said *most* kids. So if your four-year-old can't race around the driveway on his bike yet, don't panic. Most pediatricians will check your child's gross motor skills at annual checkups and advise you if there are any issues. Of course, if you feel something isn't quite right with your child's development, consult the doctor and/or teacher for a reality check. If your child's preschool has a school nurse, start there.

Uses utensils to eat. Most three-year-olds can use a fork or spoon. They can also hold a pencil between their thumb and forefinger and, milestone charts often insist, pour from a pitcher into a glass or cup.

Get real: Okay, my boys definitely weren't pouring anything into cups, even at age four, and using a correct pencil grip took them a while, too. When my son had fine motor problems, we did invest in a booklet called, "Handwriting without Tears," and a special rubber grip to make it easier for little hands to hold pencils, but it was a real chore for him until his hands suddenly started working well. Again, it comes down to how much these things bother you. Understanding that kindergarten could be tough for a kid who can't do these things, you might want to talk to the preschool teacher about it and then follow your gut. That's what I did.

 WE ASKED: What were your biggest concerns about preschool?

My child wouldn't follow instructions: 33%

Follows a two- or three-part command. Your preschooler should be able to understand and follow through on commands such as, "Go get your shoes, bring them to me, and sit down in that chair."

Get real: If she's engrossed in *Dragon Tales* when you say your command, don't expect much. Even my tweens don't follow through when I ask them to do something while they're busy. (Same goes for my husband, who generally listens to me up to the verb.) So before you panic that your preschooler has a hearing or comprehension problem, make sure you have her undivided attention.

WE ASKED: What do you wish someone had told you about parenting a preschooler?

"Potty training is not all it's cracked up to be. Try carrying a screaming frog through downtown on Halloween, desperately searching for a public toilet because she's 'too big' to wear a pull-up now, all the while cursing your husband who 'had to work' and hoping no one is going to try to arrest you for kidnapping."

—Jennifer, Puyallup, Washington

Is potty trained. Yep, most kids are potty trained by age three.

Get real: That's fine if it isn't your kid refusing to sit on the potty well past his third birthday. But we moms all know of stubborn preschoolers who have their own timetables for potty training. Meanwhile, your mother is reminding you that she had you and your brother trained by fourteen months, and the preschool registration deadline is looming. It's a lot of pressure, and it's for a reason. Chances are, if your child has no physical disabilities, he really *can* go on the potty. He just won't.

If your three- or four-year-old pretty much tells you, "I don't care. I'll sit in poop," you need to change the power structure. Sure, you could put her in underpants with the hopes that she'll feel uncomfortable enough to use the toilet, but she'll just ruin your couch and keep on watching *Wonder Pets!* The important issue is to avoid a power struggle with her. She's in charge of her body and not much else, so she might be getting a charge out of being in charge. Or she hasn't learned yet to be repulsed by poop. (She might think of it as, *Look what I made!*) She could start to withhold her poop and wind up constipated.

Instead, keep her hydrated and feed her plenty of fiber to keep the, uh, trains leaving the station. Then, give her the power she seems to crave. Tell her, "Your pee and poop are up to you now." And then stop nagging her. Once she has the responsibility to potty train, she just

> **Okay, I admit it. . . .**
>
> "My daughter was slow to speak, which leaves me worried about her future progress."
>
> —*Jill, Toledo, Ohio*

might use it. Add a time-limited privilege, such as time to play Webkinz, and you may see success—usually, but not always, within three weeks.

Puts together four- and five-word sentences. By age three, your preschooler should be able to say such gems as, "That's a big doggie" and "I want ice cream." ("Please" would be a nice bonus.)

Get real: Keep in mind that some kids are chattier than others. My mom says I didn't talk much when I was little, because I had a "spokes-brother" who talked on my behalf: "Jennifer wants a snack." And yet, I grew up to be a writer. Go figure. My older son didn't talk as much as my younger son, who can best be described as the deputy mayor of his preschool class—he was buddies with everyone. But there are some very real issues you need to look into if you suspect that your preschooler's delayed speech is something serious. Check with your preschooler's teacher and your pediatrician, who will likely refer you to specialists in speech issues.

Completes large-piece puzzles with three or four pieces. This is more a cognitive issue than a fine motor test. Your three-year-old should be able to figure out how the pieces go together.

Get real: This doesn't mean you should panic if your preschooler shows no interest in puzzles. And it's a different issue altogether if he can't hold the pieces or snap them together. This milestone is all about the ability to think through *how* to put a puzzle together. If your preschooler can't seem to grasp the way to put together a simple puzzle, look into it.

Separates easily from parent(s). Many milestone charts say that your preschooler should be able to leave you for preschool, Grandma's, or a playdate without theatrics.

Get real: My first son wouldn't stay for aftercare at preschool, even just one day a week, while my younger son asked for extra days. It's just that some kids are simply clingier than others. And three is young. It really is. So I have a hard time believing this is a big issue at this age—until you endure it every single morning at day care or preschool drop-off. If your preschooler is experiencing separation anxiety, check your own anxiety at the door first. Then take these steps to ease everyone's fears:

1. **Talk about what's going to happen.** Tell your preschooler where he's going, who will take care of him, where you're going, and when you'll be back, so he doesn't fill in the blanks with scary scenarios.

2. **Get the teacher involved.** Often, preschool teachers have little tricks to making the transition go more smoothly.

3. **Say good-bye and mean it.** If you say "bye-bye" and then stick around, you're teaching your preschooler that good-bye is negotiable. Treat it like pulling off a Band-Aid: say

your good-byes quickly, and get the heck out of there.

Can dress and undress. By age four, your preschooler should be able to put on and take off her own clothes and shoes, though lace tying will come later.

Get real: Taking off clothes, or at least pulling down pants, is an essential ability for potty training, which most kids complete by age three. But putting on clothes? Well, it depends on the clothes. Keep them simple—pull-on shirts, zipper flies, one or two buttons rather than a whole line of them. I know there's a lot of pressure to get kids to learn to tie their shoes by kindergarten, but as far as I'm concerned, that's why God gave us Velcro. If you decide to teach your preschooler to tie his shoes, use flat, fairly long (but not unwieldy), uncoated laces because they're easiest for little fingers to maneuver.

Can draw a person with two to four parts. By age four to five, your preschooler should be able to draw at least a head and body. The more body parts, the more mature educators will perceive him.

Get real: This one still churns my stomach. When my son took a kindergarten readiness exam, he tested young on his person drawing, because he pretty much stuck a circle on another blob, added two eyes and called it a day. To the educators who administered the test, this was a sign that he was less mature than other

> **Okay, I admit it. . . .**
>
> "I'm delighted when she appears before me, dressed and ready to go out, instead of whining to have me put her socks and shoes on for her."
>
> —*Elizabeth,*
> *Lansing, Michigan*

kids his age. And yet, now that he's a schoolwide renowned artist, he still hates drawing people. Please don't start cramming for kindergarten by forcing your preschooler to draw anatomically correct people. When it's time, it'll come.

WE ASKED: What did you do to prepare your child for kindergarten?

"Kumon, which we later decided was a waste of time and money."

—*Megan, Houston, Texas*

Identify some letters from the alphabet. By age five, your preschooler should be able to identify a few upper and lower case letters.

Get real: Do you find yourself frantically holding up flash cards or treating *Sesame Street* like a study session as you try to cram as much information about the ABCs, 123s, and more before kindergarten starts? Being able to identify some letters is among some of the many signs that the preschool will use to determine your child's readiness for kindergarten. Chances are, your child will learn enough letters at preschool to be prepared, but you can help at home with some simple games or simply by reading books together every night.

Wacky Preschooler Behavior and What to Do (and Not to Do) About It

YOU THOUGHT YOUR toddler acted strangely, but you figured that your preschooler, who seems to have a higher level of reasoning abilities coupled with the gift of language, should act more rationally. Still, sometimes he just doesn't, and that surprises you. There are

Okay, I admit it. . . .

"Most days, the nonstop chatter and endless questions of my five-year-old drive me insane."

—*Michelle, Azusa, California*

indeed a few behaviors that, though seemingly odd to you, are actually common among preschoolers. Here are a few.

My Preschooler Talks to Herself

You hear your preschooler talking in the other room and you begin to hope that she's chatting with the dog rather than talking to herself. But no, she's at it again. Your stomach does a little flip as you picture her thirty years from now, pushing a shopping cart full of junk up a city street, ranting about how the CIA can read her mind.

Don't worry. If your preschooler talks to herself, it's not only normal, it's good for her. Self-chatting is common among preschoolers, who use it as a transitional period after learning to talk. You may find that your child's self-chat picks up when she starts preschool. That's because she might need it to help her adjust to the challenges of school.

Again, don't worry. Self-chatting is normal among preschoolers. Besides, it's really fun to listen to.

WE ASKED: What was the worst part about having a pre-schooler?

"How opinionated they become. And stubborn. Like refusing to eat cereal out of the *blue* bowl. Only the *red* bowl will suffice. Duh, Mom."

—*Sarah, Northbridge, Massachusetts*

My Preschooler Is Stubborn!

I've heard of age four being described as two with attitude. Some preschoolers take the "my way or the highway" attitude, using their increasingly apt verbal skills to their advantage by making crazy demands or refusing to comply with what, to you, seems like normal everyday requests.

If this sounds like your preschooler (and it sounds like one of mine), I'm not going to tell you not to worry. This must drive you bonkers. And you don't have to stand for it. Here are a few ways to deal with the stubborn preschooler:

1. **Give him a small choice.** Let him choose between wearing this shirt or that one, even though you really don't care one way or another. It gives him a sense of power that he probably craves.

2. **Follow through on your threats.** If you tell your pre-

schooler she's going to have to leave the playdate if she keeps acting up, take her home if she misbehaves—even if you have to pick her up to get her out. Otherwise, she's going to keep on trying to get away with her stubbornness.

3. **Never give in on rules affecting safety and health.** He may refuse to wear his seat belt, but the car isn't going anywhere—and neither is he— until it's on.

4. **Choose your battles.** Not everything is worth a fight. If she insists on wearing her clothes to bed tonight, just let her. Unless, of course, they're muddy or filled with food, what's it to you?

Okay, I admit it. . . .

"I have no idea why the sky is blue, why some cats look alike but they're not twins, and stuff like that. I used to feel very smart, but now, not so much."

—*Helene, Stockton, California*

WE ASKED: What do you wish someone had told you about parenting a preschooler?

"Remember, preschool is supposed to be fun. Don't worry if they're not reading at three."

—*Megan, Houston, Texas*

Gimme a break

Playing Is Your Preschooler's Work

A MommaSaid fan told me the story of a four-year-old who spent a Friday night at her brother's baseball game doing worksheets while all the other kids played. The preschooler's mother explained that she wanted her daughter to get a leg up on the other kids. But her daughter probably would have learned about socialization, interacting with others, and maybe bugs, if she had been allowed to play with the other kids. Book smarts aren't the only assets your preschooler will need. Between three and five, your preschooler also needs to learn how to get along with others. Help her reach that milestone by letting play be your preschooler's work.

Just a minute!

Preschool Age Milestone Charts
(According to the Moms in Your Playgroup)

Age	Milestone
36 months	Potty trained, even through the night and on long car trips involving the consumption of copious amounts of water (no sugar here!) and bowel-juggling fruit.
39 months	Rides bicycle with no training wheels. Also, qualified to train for the X-Games.
42 months (a.k.a. 3½)	Not only can speak in full sentences that are understandable to adults, but can recite the Gettysburg Address (from memory).
45 months	Draws Renoir replicas in spare time.
48 months (you know, 4)	Completes simple puzzle. Also, 1,000-piece puzzle depicting the ocean—at night—before Grandma could get her hands on even one piece.
51 months	Potty trains younger cousin—in one day!
54 months (4½)	Has imaginary friends . . . who gather daily in the playroom to try to solve the Middle East peace dilemma.
57 months	Conjugates verbs correctly—in Farsi and Czech, too.
Let's just call it 5, okay?	Aces kindergarten readiness test. Also, *New York Times* crossword puzzle. (Saturday's, even).

Chapter Four

Soccer Moms (the Early Years)
How to Handle Your Preschooler's Ever-Expanding Social Calendar Without Permanently Moving into Your Minivan

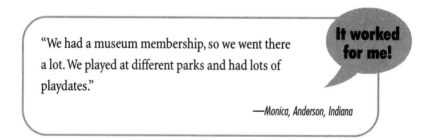

"We had a museum membership, so we went there a lot. We played at different parks and had lots of playdates."

It worked for me!

—*Monica, Anderson, Indiana*

By the time my kids were in preschool, "stay-at-home mom" had become an oxymoron for me. Some days, we were more often out than we were home, heading to the playground, Playorama class, playdates, playgroups, and even kiddie soccer, even though they were so little, their soccer jerseys fit more like dresses. I didn't care. We needed to get out.

But I drew the line at signing them up for every brain-building, good-for-socialization opportunity that came our way. I didn't think my kids had to have their every moment filled with fun yet educational activities. I just thought we should get out of the house, so they wouldn't clobber each other so much. Besides, I really needed to talk to grown-ups.

So I created a balance of playdates (they're free!) and a smattering of age-appropriate activities that helped my preschoolers let off some steam while keeping them entertained long enough for me to remain seated for more than a few minutes at a time. Here's how you can keep control of your preschooler's busier-by-the-year schedule without going (too) crazy.

Okay, I admit it. . . .

"It was easier to take a toddler to where you want to go and what you want to do as opposed to my preschooler, who's already trying to go and do what she wants."

—*Maria, Arlington, Texas*

So Much to Do, So Little Time

IN HINDSIGHT, MAYBE kiddie soccer was a bit much for my four- and five-year-olds. I mean, really, I had to rush from the school to pick up some bagels for lunch, and then to the field, where I wrestled my sons and, invariably, a friend or two, into their shin guards and cleats, while the kids managed to get cream cheese in my hair. All so they could wander around the field like bumble bees over a spilled lemonade, while we moms sat nearby and called this frenzied activity soccer. But it wasn't soccer. It was organized chaos. Still, it sweated the crankies out of my kids, let us moms relax a bit for half an hour, and made all of us sleep rather well at night. All in all, it was sixty bucks well spent.

But how do you know what activity—if any—is right for your preschooler? It all depends on your schedule, your preschooler's temperament, your other kids, and how badly you need to get out of the house. Here are my basic rules for after-school activities for preschoolers:

1. **Pick something that suits their temperaments.** I don't know what made me think that my kids would sit down and play the cymbals for music class when they rarely sat at all, let alone to jam out with a bunch of three-year-olds. That's how I wound up chasing my kids as they dashed out the door and into the hallway. That's also how we wound up as music class dropouts— twice. But when I found activities that better suited their, ahem, active lifestyle, we all enjoyed ourselves a lot more.

2. **Don't ask your preschooler, tell her.** You've signed up your three-year-old for a ballet class because (a) she likes to dance, and (b) all her friends are signed up already. Don't go and blow it by asking her if she'd like to take a ballet class. She has no concept of what the heck a ballet class entails, and, if she's in a mood, she just might say she doesn't want to go. And then you've either got a fight on

your hands, or you're out seventy bucks. Instead, before you leave, tell her, "We're going to go dance with Emily, Isabella, Emma, and Olivia!" See? It's all in the delivery.

3. **Don't schedule back-to-back activities.** You've got plenty of years ahead of you of racing from travel soccer to travel lacrosse, so why start the madness now? Besides, preschoolers aren't ready for that kind of involvement. Running through the parking lot at gymnastics—because you have to get to art class right now!—is no way to spend an afternoon with your kids, who'd probably be happier throwing rocks into a hole in your backyard anyhow.

"My preschooler takes swim lessons and preschool gym, but only one thing at a time. It is important to not be running around all the time, especially at this age. Simple lives, calm kids."

It worked for me!

—*Jen, Fort Thomas, Kentucky*

"All of my kids played soccer, some took karate, some danced. These were good for social reasons and exercise, but you get the crazy parents who think their children's soccer ability at age four will get them into the college of their dreams. Be careful not to get too intense!"

It worked for me!

—*Stephanie, East Northport, New York*

How Much Is Too Much?

WHEN I WAS in preschool, pretty much the only organized activity available to me was ballet. It took just one recital watching my future soccer player thighs bound across in pink tights for my parents to realize that perhaps I wasn't cut out for ballet. But at least I got to wear the tutu to my friend Kristen's birthday party. Yay!

Nowadays, however, there's a whole lot more than ballet for preschoolers to participate in. And with the pressure to practically prepare your preschooler for a future at Yale and, perhaps, in Major League Baseball, it's easy to get caught up in the after-school mania. But is your preschooler ready? Consider this: your preschooler still has a lot of maturing to do. Here's where kids usually stand between the ages of three and five:

Motor skills. They're still working on their ability to jump, balance, and throw. Ever watch a T-ball game? It's like watching tiny drunks attempt to play ball.

Hand-eye coordination. Their vision is still developing, and they have a hard time following speeding objects, like the soccer ball heading toward their face.

Attention span. "Look! There's a butterfly!"

Maturity. It takes kids years to develop the maturity required for proper team etiquette. Heck, some grown-ups never seem to grasp it. It's hard for preschoolers to understand why it's okay for another kid to steal the ball from her on the soccer field when that's not okay on the playground, so don't expect your preschooler to fully grasp the game's rules.

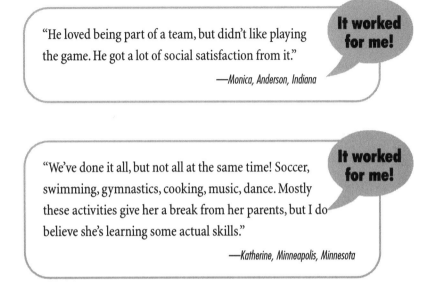

"He loved being part of a team, but didn't like playing the game. He got a lot of social satisfaction from it."

—Monica, Anderson, Indiana

It worked for me!

"We've done it all, but not all at the same time! Soccer, swimming, gymnastics, cooking, music, dance. Mostly these activities give her a break from her parents, but I do believe she's learning some actual skills."

—Katherine, Minneapolis, Minnesota

It worked for me!

Activities for Tots

STILL, AN ORGANIZED activity can be a nice way to get out and have some fun. It's a matter of finding the right one for your child. Here are the pros and cons of some of the most common preschool sports and activities to help you decide which is right for your child:

Soccer

Take it from this soccer coach, preschool-level soccer is really nothing more than a bunch of kids randomly chasing a ball around the field until someone kicks it out or accidentally scores while player is busy picking dandelions in goal.

Pros: Lots of running, which is great for the heart and a good night's sleep.

Cons: Overzealous coaches (and a few parents) can expect too much from kids who are truly too young to grasp that it's not okay to sit on the ball and ask Mommy for water in the middle of a game.

Martial Arts

I love to watch the really little kids in white karate outfits run around at our local martial arts facility. It looks like fun, and the classes are fairly organized and brief.

Pros: Lots of movement, but not chaotic. Kids learn respect and restraint while getting some nice exercise.

Cons: Some teachers expect too much, too young. Preschoolers aren't coordinated enough for complicated kicks, and they really shouldn't learn the more violent aspects of the sport until they're more mature. Classes can also get expensive.

Dance

Who doesn't want her daughter to be the next Shirley Temple? Even boys now get involved in dance classes, especially at young ages. Preschoolers can learn everything from ballet to tap and even hip-hop.

Pros: It's great exercise and a talent your preschooler will be able to use the rest of his or her life. And the outfits! Girls sure love dressing up for recitals.

Cons: Classes and all those outfits can get expensive. Expect to camp out for recital tickets at some of the larger facilities. And then there's stage fright.

> "Payton enjoys gymnastics in the summer and tap/ ballet during the school year. Our rule of thumb is one activity per season. These experiences seem to help develop her sense of pride, involvement, as well as accomplishment."
>
> —*Danelle, Middleburg Heights, Ohio*

It worked for me!

Gymnastics

The Olympics' perfect ten Nadia Comaneci got her start in gymnastics in kindergarten, so why shouldn't your future gold medalist get a jump on his or her future? There's no shortage of gymnastics classes for kids even as young as three. They're so small that they don't have far to fall, right?

Pros: Here's a chance to get the tumbling off your furniture and onto a mat overseen by professionals. Plus, your preschooler will gain flexibility, strength, and balance.

Cons: Gymnastics can be a very competitive sport for even the youngest athletes. Some gymnasts have fallen prey to anorexia. And then there's Mary Lou Retton's total hip replacement at the age of thirty-seven.

T-Ball

The precursor to pitch baseball, T-ball gives kids as young as four a chance to hit the ball and run the bases like the pros, only without any measurable excitement from parent spectators.

Pros: Little kids feel like big ones when they put on a baseball glove. It's great bonding for you and your little player, giving you a reason to go out in the yard and throw the ball around. And they're so darn cute in those uniforms and "wittle cweats."

Cons: There's a lack of measurable excitement, and there's a whole lot of standing around, which prompts some kids to spend the inning drawing in the sand or staring off while absentmindedly humming. And then there are the baseball dads who act like they're coaching at Yankee Stadium. They're *four*, guys. Chill.

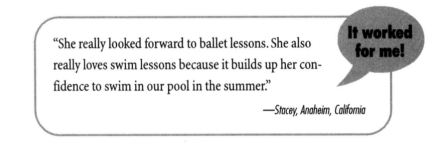

"She really looked forward to ballet lessons. She also really loves swim lessons because it builds up her confidence to swim in our pool in the summer."

—*Stacey, Anaheim, California*

It worked for me!

Swimming

Swimming is not just a sport or an activity, but a life skill that everyone should learn. Even babies take swim classes these days, but the American Academy of Pediatrics recommends that kids wait until age four to begin formal swimming lessons when they are thought to be developmentally ready.

Pros: Your preschooler will learn how to swim, which might help reduce the risk of drowning. It's fantastic exercise, and it's a lot of fun.

Cons: Unless you have your own swimming pool, you'll have to enroll early enough to beat the crowds as public pool time is limited. Plus, swim lessons can be costly. And if you're still potty training, well, warm pool . . . you get the idea.

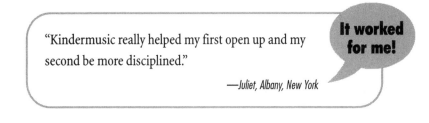

"Kindermusic really helped my first open up and my second be more disciplined."

—*Juliet, Albany, New York*

It worked for me!

Music

Your budding Mozart (or Jimi Hendrix or Madonna) gets a chance to sing and play instruments in a group setting. Or perhaps your preschooler will sign up for individual music lessons.

Pros: Your preschooler will learn rhythm and the joy of making music.

Cons: Children aren't really ready for formal music lessons until they can read and sit still for half an hour at a time. Weekly lessons can be costly, not to mention the price of the instrument. Those group classes, with a dozen kids on glockenspiels and drums, can cause parental headaches. And some kids (okay, my kids) might prefer to run around rather than sit and play music.

Cooking

If your preschooler is a self-professed "cookerman" (or woman) like my son was in preschool, a cooking class is a nice way to stoke his interest. Cooking involves math, nutrition, and best of all, eating.

Pros: Your preschooler will develop a lifelong skill while learning how to measure, cut (safely), pour, crack eggs, stir, bake, and more.

Cons: Classes at some of the franchise cooking class facilities are pricey. And what preschooler wouldn't want to take a little lick of the batter made with raw eggs when the teacher's not looking?

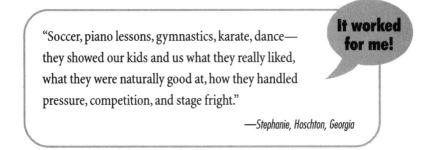

"Soccer, piano lessons, gymnastics, karate, dance— they showed our kids and us what they really liked, what they were naturally good at, how they handled pressure, competition, and stage fright."

—*Stephanie, Hoschton, Georgia*

It worked for me!

Pals and Playdates

YOUR PRESCHOOLER WILL soon forgo the parallel play of toddlerhood, when she and her friends behaved pretty much like strangers at a salad bar, and start actually playing with other kids. She might even conspire to host a playdate, which you likely won't find out about until preschool pick-up time, when suddenly, her friend Brianna announces she's coming home with you today, even though her mother is standing right there.

Okay, I admit it. . . .

"We did soccer and T-ball at four-and-a-half. Uh, well, you know, it was more of buying cleats and watching him run around and play in the dirt, caring less if the ball was coming right by him."

—*Sachia, Independence, Missouri*

But do you have Brianna over without her mom at the ready like the Secret Service at the presidential inauguration? It depends on two things: (1) is Brianna potty trained, and (2) can you stand her? That's right—I just asked you if a preschooler gets on your nerves. When your child is little, you still have ultimate control over who she hangs with and which kids get to come over to your house, so use that power while you still can.

If Brianna comes over and drives you crazy or treats your child like a nuisance that gets in her way when she just wants the dollhouse to herself, you don't have to have her over anymore. Instead, fill your preschooler's calendar yourself by setting up playdates a few days ahead of time. That way, if Brianna invites herself over, your child already has plans.

Of course, if Brianna lives next door, it's harder to keep her from popping over. Your best bet is to make house rules that she—and all playdates—must abide by. They break a rule, they go home. I've sent kids home for sliming the cat and bullying my son. One child was invited back with the promise of better behavior. The other never came over again. My son didn't want him to, nor did I.

Playdates for preschoolers are a little different than the chaos that is a toddler playdate. For one thing, they actually acknowledge each other beyond fighting over another toy or sharing an interest in putting pretzels in the dog bowl. And there's the possibility of a drop-off playdate—no escort needed. More on that later. First, here are five rules to holding playdates for your preschooler:

1. **Keep it simple.** You're not planning a rehearsal dinner. It's just a playdate. All you really need to make a playdate successful is more than one preschooler, some toys, a few snacks, and a free afternoon.

2. **Find out what your playdate can't or won't eat.** We have a young neighbor who's so allergic to peanuts, I wipe down my counters and tables before he comes over. He also can't eat dairy or chocolate. I make sure I keep on hand safe foods he can eat, so I don't wind up frantically trying to read labels while the kids are racing through my house, shouting something about paint and hammers. (Huh? Hey!) And then there are the personal likes and dislikes. One of my sons' friends ate only jelly—no peanut butter—and another wouldn't touch juice boxes. Plan snack time ahead of the playdate to make things easier on you.

3. **Resist the urge to be the entertainment director.** If you micromanage your kids' playdates, they'll never learn how to entertain themselves. Let your preschooler and his friend figure out for themselves what to play and how. Of course, if they're fighting, if someone's hurt, or if it's eerily quiet because they're coloring the dog Clifford-red just as you suspected, by all means, jump in. Otherwise, just let them play.

4. **Oversee without hovering.** Let the kids play in another (childproofed) room, but listen in as much as possible. I often folded laundry or paid bills quietly nearby, so I could

hear when things went awry. Besides, it's a lot of fun to listen to preschoolers talk to each other.

5. **Keep it short.** Anything longer than two hours is generally too darn long at this age. They tend to get tired or on each other's nerves when playdates drag on, so cut it off while the mood is still upbeat, and everyone is still friends.

WE ASKED: What's the best part about having a preschooler?

"I love how they are just developing their own little personality and their conversational skills and socialization skills."

—*Nicole, Howell, New Jersey*

To Drop-Off or Not to Drop-Off— That Is the Question

Okay, I admit it. . . .

"They just seem to be so grown up at times. They also seem to see the world outside of their own little worlds."

—*Sachia, Independence, Missouri*

AT SOME POINT, your preschooler will be ready to go to a friend's house without you in tow. But how do you know it's time for the big drop-off?

When your preschooler is potty trained. And I don't mean kinda, sorta potty trained, like how she can make it through two-and-a-half hours of preschool without an accident, but starts jonesing for her Pull-Ups and a good poop behind the dining room table at 2:00 PM. Unless you've got a very close friend or a relative with kids the same age who'll host a drop-off playdate, don't expect someone else to handle a potty clean-up.

When your preschooler is independent enough to leave you. If he's the type of kid who barely looked back at preschool drop-off since the first day of school, he's ready for a solo playdate. If he's a little more shy but knows his playdate and his playdate's caregiver fairly well, it's time, too. But if it's going to be a teary affair, you might want to attend the playdates for a while, or host a drop-off at your house until he's ready for one himself.

When you're ready for some time apart. If you're going to hide in the hedges or call every ten minutes for a status report, you're only going to give your preschooler the feeling that you don't trust her or her playdate's family. And you're going to tick off the other parents. If you can't bear to be apart, start small, with a short drop-off playdate. Give the other parent your cell phone and home phone numbers and then be patient. If, God forbid, something terrible happens, believe me, someone will call you. Meanwhile, enjoy the break . . . if you can.

When you trust the other parent. It's best to start out with someone you know well, such as a neighbor, a relative, or a long-time friend. But if you're new to a neighborhood or a school, set up a getting-to-know-you playdate with the kids and their parents first. That way, you'll be able to do some mind-easing interviewing before you leave your child with someone else. Don't hesitate to ask the questions that matter to you. If you want to know what kind of snacks are served, or whether there are guns in the house, ask. You are your child's gatekeeper, after all.

WE ASKED: What's the worst part about having a preschooler?

"Destruction. I suspect it's inherent in that age group. They have more dexterity and reasoning abilities at three or four, and they use them in really creative ways. Just ask my furniture."

—*Stephanie, Hoschton, Georgia*

"All of these activities gave them a lot of self-confidence and an outlet for their energy."

—*Jamie, Hudson, Wisconsin*

It worked for me!

Gimme a break

Don't Overschedule Your Preschooler.

Be careful not to fall into the activity trap that affects so many families these days. When it comes to after-school activities, your preschooler really needs nothing more than a little socialization and a chance to burn off some of that energy that you wish you could bottle and gulp down with your coffee. Remember, you're raising a child, not building a resume.

Just a minute!

Preschooler's Calendar,
Then and Now

	Back in the Day (When You Were Little)	**Now**
6:30 AM	Wake up. Watch cartoons until Mommy gets up.	Nudge Mommy out of bed next to you. Prepare to be entertained.
7:00 AM	Eat a bowl of Lucky Charms in front of the TV.	Help Mommy prepare nutritious breakfast from organic foods, using skills such as measuring, counting, identifying colors, and whisking.
8:00 AM	Put on outfit Mommy laid out and brush teeth.	Try to decide between the pink outfit from GapKids or the purple one from Bloomies.
9:00 AM	Circle time at the preschool.	Circle time at the preschool.
9:30–10:30 AM	Free playtime.	Phonics, math sheets, and Junior Einstein science project.

10:30 AM	Snack time (pretzels and Kool-Aid).	Snack time (individually packed snacks from list of approved food items, including apple slices, carrots, and other things that will be secretly fed to the class gerbil).
11:00–12:00 AM	Show and tell, followed by free playtime on the playground.	Show and *share*, followed by organized (get those hearts pumping!) exercise activity on the playground.
12:00 PM	Go home.	Go home or stay for "enrichment activities" involving art, music, and cooking class in thirty minute rotations.
12:30 PM	Lunch.	Lunch, between rotations.
1:00 PM –dinnertime	Free playtime.	Playgroup, karate class, soccer practice, and worksheets.
"Dinner"	"The Pizza guy is here!"	Whatever's on the cover of this month's Bon Appétit
After dinner –bedtime	Free playtime, bath, book, bed.	Free playtime, bath, allotted reading time, weasel way into Mommy's bed again.

Chapter Five

Beyond *Because I Said So!*
Putting the Kibosh on Bad Behavior

I thought I'd gotten away with something. My firstborn skipped the terrible twos altogether. Hurray! Lucky me. And then he turned three and put "no" at the top of his list of favorite words. By the time he was four, he no longer just said no. Rather, he collapsed to the ground as though his bones had disintegrated anytime I asked him to do something he didn't like to do. I tried time-outs. I tried taking away his favorite toys. I even tried the smiley face system, where I'd cross out one of three smiley faces on a piece of paper every time he misbehaved. For some reason, little kids hate to see smiley faces defaced—but he apparently didn't hate it enough.

Okay, I admit it. . . .

"The worst part is the mouthiness. Sure, she's more verbal, but she's also learned to express her attitudes, and it's not always very nice. For every 'I love you, Mommy,' there's also an 'I hate you, Mommy. You're not my friend anymore,' or 'You're not the boss of me.'"

—*Elizabeth, Lansing, Michigan*

Ultimately, I turned to professional help. I hired a parenting coach to drop by my house and pretend to take measurements for some construction work while surreptitiously taking notes on my interactions with my son. When I later told the parenting coach that my four-year-old hadn't acted up in front of him as much as he normally did, he said that kids often tone it down in front of company. "It's like a monster truck," he explained. "He wasn't going anywhere, but his engine was revving up, and I knew what he was capable of doing."

Okay, I admit it. . . .

"I wish someone had told me how much she would suddenly try to negotiate every command I give her. You teach toddlers to obey, and since their verbal skills aren't quite developed, you can get them to listen a little quicker. Now it's all about 'Just one more time, Mom.'"

—*Jessica, Wichita, Kansas*

He gave me steps for discipline that I still use today (and will share with you in this chapter along with my own field-tested modifications). But he also gave me a sense of validation. While other parents had endured terrible twos to coast through the preschool years, I was pleased to find out that I wasn't the only mom to experience the tyrannical threes and the !$#*% fours, as I so lovingly referred to them. Best of all, there'd be no !$ #*% fives!

Crime and Punishment

SOMETIME AFTER THE invention of the ubiquitous time-out and before it became all too common for parents to treat their children like their BFF (best friend forever!), some folks started to confuse discipline with punishment. While our parents' generation seemed to have no qualms about nipping bad behaviors in the bud, today's parents tend to take a more democratic approach to discipline. But there's a problem with that: it doesn't work.

Have you ever witnessed a mom trying to oh-so-sensitively explain to her three-year-old that she "can't have the bubble gum now, honey, because you already had sweets today, and we're going to Grandma's for dessert tonight anyhow, and . . ."? But the preschooler will have none of it, blowing up right there in public, and, before you know it, the kid's got her bubble gum and even a brand-new teddy bear as a consolation prize.

If you think it was hard to discipline toddlers, wait until you try to tell a preschooler "no," and the

Okay, I admit it. . . .

"We start each day with three books to read at bedtime. If she misbehaves, a book is taken away. If she does something really good, she earns a book. So far, we've tried to get to five books (a really great day!), but today we're only at three. And there have been one or two no-book days."

—Annette, West Milford, New Jersey

Okay, I admit it. . . .

"Life with a preschooler is so much different because now they have opinions and voice those opinions, whether it's about what to eat, what to wear, or anything else that they want control over. You learn to pick your battles!"

—*Stacey, Anaheim, California*

negotiations begin. Preschoolers have two things in their arsenal that they lacked during their toddler years: great verbal skills and a frighteningly proficient ability to push your buttons. They know where you're weak and how to make it work for them.

But if you start letting your three-year-old push you around, add ten years and raging hormones, and you'll have one pushy teen on your hands. Now is the time to establish a discipline plan and stick to it, or you'll lose negotiation after negotiation until, finally, you're no longer in charge. But how?

Do Time-Outs Work?

AH, THE MAGICAL time-out, the discipline tool that's supposed to immediately quash your preschooler's bad behavior and turn him into an obedient, well-mannered child. It works like this: your offspring behaves poorly, so you pull him away and sit him in a chair, on a step, or in his room for a short period of time for a cooling-off period that's designed to make him behave better. But do time-outs really work? That all depends on your kid—and you.

Maybe time-outs worked just fine when your child was a toddler, but they're losing their effectiveness now that she's older. Or maybe your preschooler really doesn't mind much sitting alone in the other room, because then he can work on the crayon mural he's been secretly creating on the wall behind your wedding photo.

Time-outs work only for certain personalities. For others, well, you might want to think of another way to get them to behave. If any of the following profiles sound like your kid, you might want to ditch the time-out:

The Fidget. You sit her down for her time-out, and she pops back up. You sit her back down and warn her to behave, but soon, she's back up again, this time with an excuse about needing water or hearing the cat at the door. If you spend the entire time-out trying to get her to sit still, your discipline effort is losing its effectiveness while you're losing your patience.

Okay, I admit it. . . .

"I made a chart for the desired behavior, and when I catch them doing it, they get a star. I also use the anti-chart, where I give them a few tokens at the start of the day, and if they do the behavior I'm trying to eliminate, they give a token back to me. If they have all the tokens at the end of the day they can stay up fifteen minutes, have an extra book, or something like that."

—*Julie, West Chester, Pennsylvania*

The Loner. To him, it really isn't punishment to be separated from the activities. He'd rather "read" a book or talk to his stuffed animals anyhow. As a result, the time-out is a reward for bad behavior. The Loner thinks, "Hey, if I smack my annoying sister, I'll get to be alone for a while!" Thwack!

The Troublemaker. She spends her time-out getting into more trouble, perhaps by scuffing up the floor with her black patent leather shoes, throwing things, or singing "The Diarrhea Song." Now you've got to give her a time-out for misbehaving during her time-out, and she doesn't care. She just wants to get a rise out of you, and it's working.

If any of these sound like your preschooler, you might want to find another punishment that better suits his temperament. I've listed more below.

It worked for me!

"He wants his way all the time and is very vocal about it, so I put his trains in time-out, taking them away for a while. This always does the trick without focusing negative attention on him."

—Melanie, Booneville, Arkansas

It worked for me!

"I count backward from five. If she isn't doing what she was told by the time I get to 'one' then she goes to time-out. It took a couple of time-outs for her to believe me. Now, I just say 'five' and she moves."

—Shelley, Travis AFB, California

How to Get the Most out of Time-Outs

If you'd like to try time-outs, or if you're wondering why they aren't working for you, consider these tips for successful time-outs:

1. **Decide which behaviors are misdemeanors and which are felonies beforehand.** Before you institute time-outs (or any behavior modification plan, really), decide which types of behaviors are bad enough to warrant time-outs. That way you won't have to decide whether to haul off your preschooler to a time-out while he's in the middle of mouthing off to you at grandma's.

2. **This isn't the time to rant, scream, and shout.** Time-outs work best if you *unemotionally* tell your preschooler what she's done wrong and then put her in a time-out. This means that you don't say things like "How many times do I have to tell you. . . ." or "You're just like you're father!" Rather, you defuse the situation and redirect her attention by providing a quiet spot for her (and you) to calm down.

3. **Don't set up the time-out in the middle of a fabulously fun spot.** A time-out in the middle of the playroom is less effective than, say, a time-out in the dining room. The stairs, the front hallway, a corner in the kitchen are all the kind of unfun spots that are ideal for time-outs. I'd suggest you avoid sending your preschooler to his room for the same reason.

4. **Find your emergency time-out locations for when you're on the go.** As soon as you enter someone else's home, a store, or anywhere other than your house, choose a spot for time-outs, so you're not frantically dragging a screaming preschooler through the lingerie department at Macy's, looking for a good time-out spot. Also, decide how you'll

handle bad behavior when you're in the car. Momma always said, "I'm gonna stop this car, right now!" If you say it, mean it. And then follow through.

5. **Time it right.** If it's too short, it won't work, and if it's too long, your preschooler might stop being ticked off and start being resentful, plotting her revenge upon you, the meanest mommy on Earth. A good rule of thumb for time-outs is one minute for each year of their age. For preschoolers, that's three to five minutes tops.

6. **Revisit the infraction when it's over.** After the time-out is over and your preschooler is (hopefully) calmer, tell him why he got the time-out in the first place, so he starts to learn what kinds of behaviors will land him in a time-out.

7. **Stick to your guns.** If you skip a time-out, your preschooler just might make a mental note of it. Then, the next time you threaten a time-out, she'll keep acting up, figuring it's worth it in case you decide to skip the punishment again this time. Be consistent no matter how dog tired you are or how fed up you are with disciplining, or you'll pay for it later.

> **It worked for me!**
>
> "We had very few issues with my shy daughter, but my outgoing son was very 'busy,' and we had problems with him hitting other kids. Time-outs were used, as well as privileges being revoked."
>
> —Jamie, Hudson, Wisconsin

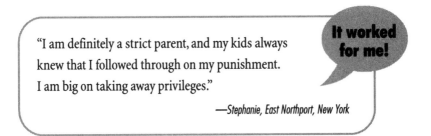

"I am definitely a strict parent, and my kids always knew that I followed through on my punishment. I am big on taking away privileges."

—*Stephanie, East Northport, New York*

¡Adios, Dora!
Removing Privileges as Consequences

EVEN NOW THAT my kids are older, taking away privileges as a consequence for bad behavior works. When one kid smacks his brother, he loses his dessert, a playdate, or access to the Wii for a period of time. It worked well when they were preschoolers, too. But there's an art to making this method of discipline work, and if you don't plan it out right, it could backfire. Here are some of the rules for making removing privileges work in your home:

1. **Get your kid to help you pick out the privilege to remove.** Really. It works. I learned this from that parenting expert I hired. He was big on removing privileges, but said it only works when it matters to your child. So when things were calm one evening, I asked my preschooler to come up with a consequence that seemed fair to him. You'd think he would have cheated, saying, "Take away my broccoli." Instead, he suggested I remove his favorite toy trucks. That way, he bought into my approach to discipline, thereby making it work better than if I had chosen the consequences myself.

2. **Threaten once and then follow through.** Have you ever watched a mom repeatedly threaten to take away her kid's candy/toy/ball/stuffed animal, only to skip following through? That's exactly what her child was counting on, and so the kid didn't behave. Removing privileges works only if you actually remove the privilege. I like to give one warning first before I swoop in and follow through on my threat. With enough practice, all you need is the warning to stop the bad behavior.

3. **Do it in public.** You're at Walmart, but the toys you've promised to take away if your kid misbehaves are at home. You need some on-the-go consequences you can use in a pinch. If you promised an ice cream after you shop, un-promise it. Put the beach ball you just put in your cart back on the shelf. Skip the trip to the playground on the way home. Whatever it is, make it work for you while you're out, because waiting to get home to punish the bad behavior that occurred while you were out loses its effectiveness with preschoolers, who may forget what the fuss was about by the time you get to the consequence.

4. **Tweak your plan as needed.** Eventually, your preschooler will lose interest in the very thing you've threatened to take away. When the trading cards, dolls, or bubble gum lose their appeal with your kid, change the consequence so it keeps on working for you.

READER/CUSTOMER CARE SURVEY

HEFG

We care about your opinions! Please take a moment to fill out our online Reader Survey at **http://survey.hcibooks.com.**
As a **"THANK YOU"** you will receive a **VALUABLE INSTANT COUPON** towards future book purchases
as well as a **SPECIAL GIFT** available only online! Or, you may mail this card back to us.

(PLEASE PRINT IN ALL CAPS)

First Name		MI.		Last Name

Address				City

State	Zip			Email

1. Gender
- ☐ Female   ☐ Male

2. Age
- ☐ 8 or younger
- ☐ 9-12   ☐ 13-16
- ☐ 17-20   ☐ 21-30
- ☐ 31+

3. Did you receive this book as a gift?
- ☐ Yes   ☐ No

4. Annual Household Income
- ☐ under $25,000
- ☐ $25,000 - $34,999
- ☐ $35,000 - $49,999
- ☐ $50,000 - $74,999
- ☐ over $75,000

5. What are the ages of the children living in your house?
- ☐ 0 - 14   ☐ 15+

6. Marital Status
- ☐ Single
- ☐ Married
- ☐ Divorced
- ☐ Widowed

7. How did you find out about the book?
(please choose one)
- ☐ Recommendation
- ☐ Store Display
- ☐ Online
- ☐ Catalog/Mailing
- ☐ Interview/Review

8. Where do you usually buy books?
(please choose one)
- ☐ Bookstore
- ☐ Online
- ☐ Book Club/Mail Order
- ☐ Price Club (Sam's Club, Costco's, etc.)
- ☐ Retail Store (Target, Wal-Mart, etc.)

9. What subject do you enjoy reading about the most?
(please choose one)
- ☐ Parenting/Family
- ☐ Relationships
- ☐ Recovery/Addictions
- ☐ Health/Nutrition
- ☐ Christianity
- ☐ Spirituality/Inspiration
- ☐ Business Self-help
- ☐ Women's Issues
- ☐ Sports

10. What attracts you most to a book?
(please choose one)
- ☐ Title
- ☐ Cover Design
- ☐ Author
- ☐ Content

TAPE IN MIDDLE; DO NOT STAPLE

BUSINESS REPLY MAIL
FIRST-CLASS MAIL PERMIT NO 45 DEERFIELD BEACH, FL

POSTAGE WILL BE PAID BY ADDRESSEE

NO POSTAGE
NECESSARY
IF MAILED
IN THE
UNITED STATES

Health Communications, Inc.
3201 SW 15th Street
Deerfield Beach FL 33442-9875

FOLD HERE

Comments

5. **Be consistent, even if it hurts for now.** If you punish your preschooler one day for smacking his sister, but let it go the next because you're under the weather, or you feel like hiding behind your newspaper, think again. You're actually creating more work for yourself later, because your preschooler has now discovered your weakness and will try to make it work for him again. And then you'll have to work even harder to make your discipline plan effective later.

WE ASKED: What discipline issues cropped up during the preschool years?

"A lot of clinginess, attitude, tantrums. I tried ignoring it, time-outs, and so on. It was a rough year."

—*Stephanie, St. Paul, Minnesota*

Okay, I admit it. . . .

"My oldest daughter is a people pleaser. She pretty much did what we asked, and we figured we had this discipline thing licked. But my youngest daughter is a tester: she needs to know exactly what will happen if she chooses to go down the wrong path so that she can decide if it's worth her while. For example: 'If you tear the wiggly eye off the felt chicken you made in school, I will not glue it back on, and the chicken will be garbage.' Two days, and thirty repeats of this statement later, she managed to pry the eye off. 'If you touch the new TV, you will not be allowed to watch it this weekend.' Fork: 1. Flat screen: 0. It's still a work in progress."

—*Jennifer, Puyallup, Washington*

The Smiley Face System

I USED THIS discipline tactic during the late-toddler and early-preschooler years, and it worked—for a while, anyhow. Here's how it works:

1. You draw or print out three smiley faces on a piece of paper.

2. You place the paper somewhere prominent, such as on the refrigerator door.

3. When your child misbehaves, you cross out one of the smiley faces. For some reason, this drives three-year-olds bonkers. They hate to see a perfectly good smiley face ruined.

4. You write the infraction underneath, even though, chances are, your kid can't read yet.

5. When all three smiley faces are crossed out, you take away a privilege.

6. You start all over.

Another variation of this plan is the happy/sad face system. You place a green smiley face on the fridge. When your child misbehaves, you replace it with a red sad face. Next to the face, you list activities your preschooler can do to replace the red sad face with the green one.

The smiley face system worked for a little while for me, but eventually my kids didn't care about the smiley faces so much anymore. I crossed them out, and they shrugged.

Still, it set the stage for the privilege removal plan by teaching my kids that discipline was a part of our daily routine, just like brushing teeth and using the potty.

What I Learned from the Parenting Expert

BY THE TIME I was frustrated enough to turn to outside help, my four-year-old's mood ruled the house. Time-outs weren't working, the smiley face system had frowned upon us, and screaming like an extra on *Saw II* was a miserable failure.

The expert taught me to modify privilege removal to suit our family's needs (and my son's rotten moods). First, I enlisted my preschooler's help. I told him that we were going to work on a new plan to make him behave better, as though I was teaching him how to ride a bike or read. I was the master, and he was the student.

He helped me brainstorm consequences that would matter to him, and, believe it or not, he picked one that I would have chosen: taking his toy trucks and cars away.

I told him we would be working on a specific goal: teaching him to accept "no" for an answer. Anytime he didn't accept "no," thereby causing him to protest, whine, rant, or drop to the ground and writhe about, he'd lose his beloved Matchbox cars or Tonka trucks for a set amount of time. Then he'd have to go to his room for a few minutes until I called him back down. If he was calm, I'd explain why he lost his cars, and, here's the hard part, he'd have to say, "Okay."

It took just a few days for him to learn to accept "no" without theatrics. If he was tired or hungry, it was harder for him to follow our plan. But all I had to do was remind him about accepting "no," and, for the most part, he sucked it up and, more important to him, kept all of his cars and trucks.

A Word About Spanking

LET'S FACE IT: the majority of parents spank their kids. Right or wrong, they do, and I'm not about to tell you not to, even though I don't do it. It just seemed silly to me to yell, "Hey, don't hit your brother!" followed by swat!

But before you spank your preschooler, consider why you're doing it. Is it an effective behavior modification program for you, or are you just plain ticked off and need a way to show it? If it's the latter, why not try some of the other discipline ideas I've outlined above, sticking with them for longer than an afternoon or until your patience runs out, and see if there isn't a better way to get your preschooler to behave? Experts say that spanking works only in the short term. In the long term, it can be problematic. But the approaches I've mentioned here have proven to have positive lasting effects—for both kids and their parents.

Gimme a break

Stick to Your Discipline Plan.

Chances are, your preschooler will ferret out who's the pushover in the family, the person most likely to cave in to her demands and temper tantrums. Whether it's Grandpa's coddling and abundant sweets or Daddy's "Aw, she's only four" dismissals, you may feel like you're the only one with the fortitude to carry through a discipline plan. Don't let their ineptitude dissuade you. If they want to teach your preschooler to disobey them, that may well be their business. But if your preschooler knows Mommy carries through with consequences, she will mind her manners around you. Once she learns how to behave around you, you can try to work on her behavior around everyone else.

"⏰ Just a minute!

Legal Complaint

Plaintiff Chloe, an individual, resident of your house, vs. Defendant Mommy and Daddy, a partnership.

Facts

Plaintiff hereby complains and states to the court that the Defendant:

1. knowingly and unlawfully presented the Plaintiff with the Big Bird bowl at breakfast this morning, despite Plaintiff's repeated request for the Blues Clues bowl.

2. advised Plaintiff that Blues Clues bowl was in the dishwasher, dirty, even though Plaintiff really couldn't care less where it was, except that it wasn't on the kitchen table where she had so clearly requested said bowl.

3. went on to serve Cheerios in the Big Bird bowl, even though Plaintiff wanted Corn Flakes and didn't want to hear anything about "shopping lists" and "time" and "tomorrow."

4. insisted on making Plaintiff eat raspberries, which obviously feel all yucky in your mouth.

5. wouldn't let Plaintiff play "Pocketful of Sunshine" from *Kidz Bop 14* CD for the eleventh time, citing something about an "aneurysm" and "Extra Strength Excedrin."

Wherefore

Plaintiff demands judgment against Defendant in excess of two (2) extra hours on Club Penguin, a shopping spree at Toys "R" Us, and choice of breakfast for the remainder of the month.

Chapter Six

In the Mix:
New Babies, Big Sibs, and Other Family Members

My brother kicked my grandmother in the shins. As far as he was concerned, she deserved it. I mean, why would Gram want anything to do with his new little sister when he was so adorable at three years old? My mother said that he demanded, "Don't you go near that baby!" I think it took him a while to get over his jealousy of me, though I swear I'm still cuter.

At just nineteen months old when his brother was born, my firstborn didn't know he was supposed to be jealous like my

Okay, I admit it. . . .

"She loves her father. It seems like I could have a circus going on in the living room, but if her father walks through the door, that is all she cares about at that moment."

—*Megan, Franklin, Maine*

85

brother had been when I was born. By the time Nicholas was in preschool, his little bro was a walking, talking toddler who stole his toys, which, of course created other issues, including explaining to a three-year-old why it's not okay to push your brother into the toy box no matter how many times he tries to walk off with the toy backhoe.

Whether you've added a baby to your family or your preschooler has older siblings, he's got to learn to deal with them. And you've got to deal not only with sibling rivalry, but Grandma's spoiling, Aunt Sarah's awful pinkapalooza outfits she keeps sending over for your little tomboy, and more. Your preschooler and your family: perfect together? Well, we'll see.

Okay, I admit it. . . .

"My daughter adores my parents. They are more kid people. My in-laws are not really kid people, so they have a hard time relating."

—*Jodie, Morton, Illinois*

Your Preschooler, Your Family, Your Sanity . . . or Lack Thereof

I DON'T THINK my sons truly bonded with their father until they were three years old. Before that, my husband simply tolerated their Cheerio-dropping, suddenly screeching, toddler mania. At age three, though, our boys could start talking "man talk" with him. And though I'm certain that our sons were not much help to him when he was trying to fill wheelbarrows and fix things around the house, at least they were more enthusiastic about it than I've ever been. After all, Hubby could sit through "There Goes a Dump Truck" without his eyes rolling into the back of his head. Me? Not so much.

My preschoolers had their favorite family members, and our family members probably had their favorite preschooler, but that's none of our business. My older son had a thing for my mother-in-law, who called him, "mein goldfogel" or "my gold bird." My younger son loved my dad, who found Christopher's smiley enthusiasm intoxicating. And my brother became a six-foot-two-inch playground for both my preschoolers.

In the middle of it all was Mommy, who managed their social calendar and their exposure to all of the relatives, except, of course, Daddy, who came home at the end of each day. As your child gets older, she'll be able to forge stronger relationships with relatives near and far. Here's the scoop on keeping it all in the family.

> **It worked for me!**
>
> "What we did was give my daughter a baby doll that was about the same size as her little brother. She was able to hold, feed, change, and be a 'mommy' to her own little baby. It was a lot of work, since I had to take care of a newborn and help the little one with her new 'baby,' but a little peace and quiet was what I got in return, and that was worth every second of extra work for me."
>
> —Diane, Schwenksville, Pennsylvania

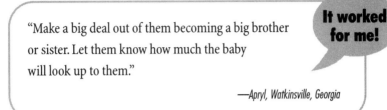

"Make a big deal out of them becoming a big brother or sister. Let them know how much the baby will look up to them."

—*Apryl, Watkinsville, Georgia*

But *I'm* the Baby in This House!

IF YOUR PRESCHOOLER is your firstborn, she was probably the "it girl" of the house until that baby showed up and ruined everything. There are many ways that your preschooler might show you her disdain for sharing the mommy love pie. Here are a few, along with tips on how to deal with them if your preschooler:

Is green with envy. Maybe your preschooler is going around kicking the shins of anyone who comes near the baby, too. Or maybe she's trash-talking the baby when neighbors drop by with baby presents. When you bring the baby home from the hospital, make sure she's not in Mommy's or Daddy's arms when you make the introductions. Just ask your preschooler if he'd like to meet his little sister (preferably when the baby's not wailing), and then bring him over to say hello.

Is jealous when the baby gets attention from visitors. Ask family members to greet your preschooler first, before the baby (who won't remember it anyway). And a little grandma swag—a gift just for your preschooler—goes a long way toward taming the green envy monster.

Tries to hurt the baby. Never leave the baby alone with your preschooler, and make sure to hover nearby, just in case. Tell your preschooler that you won't tolerate harmful behavior, and follow through with a time-out or whatever discipline tool you use. After disciplining your preschooler, make sure you assure her that you still love her just as much as before. Promise a little alone time with her as a salve for her emotional wounds.

Acts like a baby. Hey, it works for your newborn. So your preschooler figures that he ought to "tawk wike a baby," or worse, act like one by refusing to dress or feed himself or by regressing on potty training. Give your preschooler the attention he craves. Plan some one-on-one time, perhaps when the baby is sleeping or while Daddy gives your newborn a bath. Do "big kid" activities— and bill them as such—like playing board games or going to see a movie.

Wants to be your little helper. Your preschooler may take a shine to helping you out. Congratulations! You've got someone to fetch diapers and such. But be careful not to put any responsibility of unsupervised baby care on your preschooler, who's too young to truly help out like an older child can.

It worked for me!

"The little one thinks she can do everything her big sister does. I try to divert my preschooler with her own toys or, if all else fails, her *Curious George* DVD."

—Apryl, Watkinsville, Georgia

"The older one plays with the younger ones, so it's actually less work for us."

It worked for me!

—*Diane, Schwenksville, Pennsylvania*

Big Bro, Big Sis: Keeping the Peace

THANKS TO HIS big brother, my younger son had a built-in play-date from the get-go. Only nineteen months apart in age, my boys share similar interests, toys, clothes, and friends. And it's all hunky-dory until one of them wallops the other one, and I become a referee.

When my younger son was a preschooler, big bro was a kindergartener who liked to take his status as the elder, wise man and wise off, egging his playdate to help him gang up on poor little Christopher. Except "poor little Christopher" was only about two inches shorter and a few pounds lighter than Nicholas, so he could hold his own. One minute, they were all playing nicely in the backyard, and the next, somebody charged someone else's fort, and soon I had *Friday Night SmackDown* in our pachysandra.

Chances are, the older your preschooler's siblings are, the more annoying your preschooler will be deemed at various times during the day. Here are some the most common big sib–little sib issues with tips on how to handle them.

He's annoying me! Your older child is trying to do homework or watch *American Idol* without having to listen to a monologue by a five-year-old who thinks it's a great time to discuss the finer points of her new SpongeBob backpack. Fix it by:

- Separating them and giving your preschooler the one-on-one attention she's trolling for right now.

- Setting up big kid zones in the house where your preschooler isn't allowed to visit at certain times, such as the kitchen table at homework time or the living room during your older child's favorite shows.

- Making your preschooler feel like a big kid by asking him to help you cook dinner, clean out the car, or some other activity that keeps him out of his big sib's hair.

- Inviting another preschooler over for a playdate to keep her busy while your older children do their own thing.

He's touching my things! Your grade-schooler just discovered that her desk was rearranged by some grubby little hands. Worse, her favorite stuffed animal is wearing a chef's hat and a tutu. Minimize it by:

- Making a rule that your preschooler isn't allowed in her sibling's room without permission.

- Letting your older child shut the door (carefully) on your preschooler if he won't take the hint and leave.

- Not forcing your kids to share every single item. Some possessions should be personal, thereby giving your older children the autonomy they need.

- Putting breakable or expensive items out of your preschooler's reach, so that you don't find the Guitar Hero guitar covered in Crayola and Cheetos.

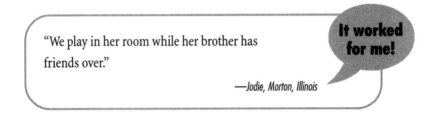

"We play in her room while her brother has friends over."

—Jodie, Morton, Illinois

It worked for me!

Do you have to bring him along? Would you have wanted a preschooler chatting up your fellow sixth-grade buddies on the way to the teen canteen? Probably not. Avoid it by:

- Leaving your preschooler with Daddy, another family member, or a neighbor when you carpool the older kids to certain events.

- Keeping your preschooler entertained at older siblings' sporting events and other places with a playdate, a game, or a nice big snack.

- Arranging special outings just for your older children so they get some big kid time with you.

- Keeping your preschooler busy with his own book, game, or toy if he's got to tag along.

"My mother and mother-in-law watch my daughter on the two days I work. She looks forward to both Monday and Wednesday, because she does different things with each grandma. She also adores both her grandpas."

It worked for me!

—*Robin, Mechanicsburg, Pennsylvania*

"My dad is wonderful with our kids. He is always willing to go outside and push them on the swing and get all the toys out of the garage. He's sometimes out there for hours!"

It worked for me!

—*Keena, Reading, Pennsylvania*

The Grands:
Grandparents and Your Preschooler

MY MOTHER HAS taught my kids the finer points of childhood, including how to blow a bubble with gum, how to throw a curve ball, and even how to spit. (Gee, thanks, Mom.) It's like she's a consultant on the set of *The Little Rascals*. Hommy, as my niece named her because she couldn't pronounce *Grammy*, is the anti-grandmother's grandma. And my boys love her for it.

While my mother-in-law loves babies, my mom likes a kid who can throw a ball. As far as she is concerned (and frankly, me, too), children don't become human until preschool. Before that, it feels more like wrangling animals at the zoo. So my mom became more (willingly) involved when my boys hit age three, thereby opening up lots of opportunities that we really didn't have before, including our first annual three-generation August trip, that summer, to Mystic, Connecticut, courtesy of Hommy.

Whether your preschooler's grandparents live nearby or across the country, there are several ways to help foster the relationship between your child and "the grands":

1. **Give them alone time.** When my kids were little, my in-laws invited my kids overnight every few weeks. It gave them time to do special stuff without us, including creating rocket ships out of boxes, going ice skating and running through the sprinkler in the backyard. And it gave my husband and me a chance to complete entire paragraphs, uninterrupted.

2. **Keep in touch if they're far away.** Even preschoolers can carry on short, albeit sometimes confusing, phone conversations. But even if no one's sure what they're talking about, it's nice for the grands to hear from your preschooler now and then. You can also send photos and videos of your preschooler in various activities, or for the tech savvy among you, have a video conference. Upload your photos onto an online site where the grands can order prints of their favorite shots, or mail a few now and then. My mother even bought me a portable photo printer so she wouldn't have to

wait (too long, anyhow) for photos of her grandsons to place in her scrapbook collection.

3. **Plan visits while you still can.** When your preschooler gets older and more involved in travel sports and other activities, it'll be harder to get away to visit. Try to arrange visits as often as you can, or have the grands visit you. If they live close, set up a regular monthly or weekly dinner, rotating houses so no one household is doing all the cleaning.

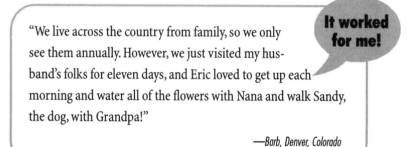

"We live across the country from family, so we only see them annually. However, we just visited my husband's folks for eleven days, and Eric loved to get up each morning and water all of the flowers with Nana and walk Sandy, the dog, with Grandpa!"

—*Barb, Denver, Colorado*

It worked for me!

When Relatives Work Against You

NOW THAT YOUR child is old enough to carry on meaningful conversations and go off without you, she may spend more time in the company of family members without you. This can be a wonderful opportunity to give your preschooler some independence under the supervision of someone you trust. But it can also mean your preschooler is going to come home with blue icing all over her face, hopped up on cupcakes (that's lunch?) and some new

Okay, I admit it. . . .

"We all have different views about parenting, and they are the type of family that loves to help. Sometimes they help too much!"

—*Megan, Franklin, Maine*

four-letter words she learned, courtesy of Uncle Bob.

So how do you handle it when your relatives actually work against you and not with you? Here are a few of the most egregious yet common issues when it comes to relatives interfering with parenting your preschooler.

They don't follow our rules for diet. You told your in-laws that you don't want your preschooler to eat cotton candy at the carnival, but they give it to her anyhow. What can you do? Certainly, if it's an issue of food allergy or sensitivity, you need to be vigilant. If your relative doesn't understand or won't respect your rules when it comes to food safety and your child, you're going to have to restrict their unfettered access to your preschooler. But if it's simply a matter of a little spoiling—some extra cookies or a hot dog instead of meatloaf for dinner—choose your battles wisely. You don't want to use food as a weapon in a war that doesn't have to be.

Their parenting styles clash with ours. Your sister won't let her kids watch TV—ever—while you're okay with a little Nick Jr. now and then. You're going to have to make some compromises when it comes to clashing parenting styles so that you meet somewhere in the middle. Call your sister to make rules that work for both of you when you're visiting her house and vice versa, or if you plan to travel together as a family. If you don't lay it out ahead of time, someone will end up ticked off, thereby turning Thanksgiving into a showdown. And who wants that?

They think our safety rules are silly. Have you heard something like this? "You didn't have a car seat, and you turned out fine." You turned out fine, sure, but perhaps you were lucky that nobody hit your mom's station wagon while you sat, seat beltless, in the backseat, making faces at the dump truck driver behind you. When it comes to safety, your rules aren't negotiable. Explain to your relative that you have done your research on car seats/bed rails/outlet covers, and so on, and you must ask them to comply or your preschooler won't be able to visit. And that's it. No compromises.

They're not good with little kids. If your relative doesn't know how to relate to a four-year-old, don't force anything on him or her. Make sure you stay close by when your preschooler is trying to

Okay, I admit it. . . .

"She is at an age where she loves anyone who will give her their undivided attention, so if cousins, aunts, uncles, or whoever gives her that attention, she is in love with them."

—*Diane, Schwenksville, Pennsylvania*

share his new toy fire truck—the one with the working sirens!—with Uncle Mike, who just wants to watch the game on TV. If your relative starts to look for an exit, help out by moving your preschooler and his truck elsewhere.

They don't invite your preschooler. If all of your preschooler's cousins are much older or a different gender, your preschooler might not get invited to certain family gatherings. Make sure you

Okay, I admit it. . . .

"Her relationship with my husband has gotten much better since I went back to work, and he's been home with her more. Needless to say, she doesn't listen to him as well as she does me, but I guess I'm the disciplinarian in the home."

—*Keena, Reading, Pennsylvania*

talk about it with your family to find a way to either include your child or create a preschooler- or boy- or girl- friendly activity everyone can do together.

Here's Daddy!

YOU COULD SPEND the entire day holding tea parties with dolls or digging with toy backhoes in the yard, and yet when Daddy walks in, it's as though Elvis has just arrived at the annual fan club meeting.

Or you could leave your preschooler with Daddy while you try to go shave your kneecaps, only to find your preschooler talking to you on the other side of the shower curtain while Daddy checks his e-mail.

On any given day, your preschooler's relationship with Daddy can be hot or cold or somewhere in between. Here are some tips to make sure everybody's getting along:

1. **Don't use the words, "Daddy is babysitting."** You can't babysit your own children. Even if you're the primary caregiver, Daddy is, well, the daddy, and not a second-rate fill-in for you. Give your husband the gift of responsibility so that your preschooler can learn to trust him (and

hopefully, go to him, so you can finish your shower).

2. **Create a dad-only activity.** When my boys were preschoolers, my husband had Saturday mornings to do dad-son things while I went to the gym. They went for haircuts, ate at the bagel shop, and wandered around Home Depot together. It gave the three of them their time together without Mom in the mix, and it was good for their relationship (and my triceps).

Okay, I admit it. . . .

"I think my daughter is closest to her father. She cries when he leaves a lot, but never does when I leave. They play games a lot when I'm away."

—*Robin,*
Mechanicsburg, Pennsylvania

3. **Don't treat Daddy like a dolt.** Dads aren't moms. They parent their own way. As long as nobody's at risk for getting hurt, don't criticize his parenting or swoop in to rescue him when you'd do something differently. As long as he isn't undoing your disciplining or potty training efforts, let him be the dad and you be the mom.

Okay, I admit it. . . .

"Eric adores his 'aunts and uncles' who are our friends here at home. Their kids are Eric's playmates and are equivalent to cousins as they are so close and have been since they were infants."

—*Barb, Denver, Colorado*

Gimme a break

Learn to Let Go

If you've been the numero uno in your preschooler's life, it can be hard to let other people take over, caring for your child and influencing his development. But good parenting is about preparing your child for a future without you. Learn to slowly let your child go by allowing family and close friends into your preschooler's life. Providing the gift of independence, confidence, and positive outside influences will help your child grow.

Just a minute!

New!

The Daddy Backyard Action Figure

Product Features:

- Fully poseable figure.
- Outfit includes fading college T-shirt with reference to beer and a party that started after what is now his bedtime.
- Wheelbarrow accessory holds realistic looking mulch and the "I Help Daddy" Preschooler Action Figure.
- Says four sentences, including:

  "Who left the bike in the bushes?"

  "Just one more tree to cut down."

  "No, no. Only Daddy can touch that."

  "You didn't tell me we were going to your sister's today!"

  "I was just resting my eyes!"
- Chain saw, riding mower, and hammock accessories sold separately.

Chapter Seven

Play D'oh!
The Ins and Outs of Entertaining a Preschooler

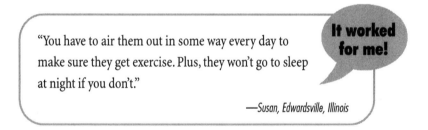

"You have to air them out in some way every day to make sure they get exercise. Plus, they won't go to sleep at night if you don't."

It worked for me!

—*Susan, Edwardsville, Illinois*

I didn't notice it until I ran the vacuum by it. How I managed to miss the plastic toy dinosaurs that one or both of my children had stuck into the dirt of one of my living room plants, I don't know. But I do know that it looked like a scene from *Journey to the Center of the Earth*. Well, except for the SpongeBob key chain, of course.

101

When my sons were preschoolers, I stumbled upon quite a few of their creative displays or the aftermath of some sort of game that, to me, made no sense. What could they possible do with a homemade black and gold cape, swim goggles, a plastic golf club, and an empty Play-Doh can? I was sure that I didn't want to know. As long as they were playing peacefully (and not sticking that Play-Doh into the spaces in our heater vents), it was fine with me.

Preschoolers have a confidence in their own clever imaginations, while older kids and adults often don't. What grown-up could show up one April afternoon at a friend's house in her brother's Spiderman halloween costume and a pair of black patent leather shoes with lacy white socks? Even if you were intoxicated, you'd eventually end up mortified.

Now that your child is a preschooler, you can likely introduce craft projects, games, and activities that would have been met with indifference by your toddler, who would rather have dipped that paintbrush in the dog's water bowl, placed it on your kitchen chair, and then wandered off. Elapsed time: three minutes.

This chapter is all about play, including—and, for mom's sake, especially—helping preschoolers learn to play on their own. You'll find out about the kinds of toys and art projects that really get preschoolers going—the ones that send their imagination swirling. Also, since younger siblings tend to covet the things their older sisters or brothers love most, I'll touch on ways to reinforce the *ask before you touch* message for your preschooler. Believe me, it'll help cut down on the older sib's ear-piercing shrieks of "Maaaa, Julia'sTouchingMyAmericanGirlDolllllll." Finally, it's not unusual for kids to start eyeballing your computer during the preschool years, so I'll talk about the appropriate ways to introduce kids to fun on the computer while starting to teach them about online safety.

Let the Games Begin

ONE OF MY favorite things about three- to five-year-olds is that they're finally old enough to follow simple rules for some very fun games. While my toddlers preferred to play peekaboo over and over and over and over and—well, you're just getting through that phase, so you know—my preschoolers liked to play Go Fish. Finally, a game with a point and, most important, a defined ending. On a long, rainy sick day, I could get out the Trouble game, and manage to entertain a cranky kid or two (and Mom) for a good twenty minutes. In preschooler time, that's at least two hours.

But, don't assume that your preschooler is ready to break out the Monopoly board and start trading in houses for hotels. If you understand where your preschooler is coming from, you'll be better able to pick the right game for her. Here are some things to know about preschoolers and the games they love to play.

They are sticklers for the rules. It always amazed me that my four-year-old couldn't remember to put his socks in the hamper, and yet he'd get fixated on one minor detail from a game of tag we'd played the week before. You know what I mean: "You said so, Mommy!" Keep the rules simple and follow them closely.

They might play in stereotypical gender ways. Try as you may, your son just doesn't want to play with dolls, or your daughter wants nothing to do with toy cars. When I left my old doll in my son's room, she ended up head-down in a dump truck, like something from a crime scene on *CSI*, only more disturbing. You can't force them to play in ways they're not interested in, so why try?

They are masters of imaginative play. They may pretend they're ice cream truck drivers, runway models, doctors, or Daddy. Help them cultivate their imaginations by supplying old clothes and various props they can use for dressing up. But don't make them adhere to your logical rules of play. If your daughter's Olympic gymnast wears a tutu and a cowboy hat, so be it.

They don't limit play to the playroom. You might not want a plastic toy explosion all over your house, and you don't have to have one. But understand that preschoolers can make a game out of your measuring cups and today's *New York Times*, too. Let them play—and then teach them how to clean it up when they're done.

They don't always want to play with educational games. You may want your preschooler to practice her ABCs or 123s, but he just wants to pretend he's an astronaut. Pretend or free play is actually very important for your preschooler's development, so make sure you give him time for it.

WE ASKED: What's the best thing about having a preschooler?

"His imagination is just wild. It's fun to watch him learn to play all on his own and have a good time."

—*Maria, Westfield, New York*

WE ASKED: What's the worst thing about having a preschooler?

"Keeping him entertained during the day, especially if the weather is bad and you can't go outside."

—Susan, Edwardsville, Illinois

What Can Your Kid Do?

WHILE YOUR TODDLER lacked fine motor skills and often reason, your preschooler is a bit more ready to play with less managing and supervision on your part. Here's what to expect from your preschooler when it comes to play.

Your three-year-old:

• Has better fine motor skills, so blocks, puzzles, and toys with movable parts are easy to play with now.

• Likes toys that have real-life sounds, like a toy phone that rings or a toy car with a working horn.

• Loves to move, so toys for pulling and pushing are often a hit.

Best toys: Stuffed animals, dolls, large-pieced puzzles, musical instruments (if you can stand them), ride-on cars, tricycles, toys that make real-life noises like toy fire trucks and dolls that cry.

Your four-year-old:

• Loves to tell jokes, even if they make no sense to you.

• Has improved gross motor skills.

• Can play board games by the rules, so you no longer have to endure an afternoon of watching your kid move the game piece straight to Queen Frostine while absentmindedly singing the theme song from *Go, Diego, Go!* for no apparent reason.

Best toys: Dress-up clothes, action figures, Barbies (if you don't mind the body issues and the ever-growing wardrobe), board games where reading isn't necessary Candy Land, I Spy for preschoolers; balls, LEGOs, kitchen sets, toy trucks and cars, and Leapster.

Your five-year-old:

• Can sit longer than ever before.

• Loves to tell stories and create things.

• Tends to get a little obsessed over things, which is why you might have to play Uno thirty-seven times this week.

Best toys: Simple arts and crafts such as finger painting or sticker projects, word or letter games that help teach reading, action figures, realistic looking dolls, sandboxes, crayons, markers, clay, matching games, role-play equipment (kitchen sets, phones, and so on), and bikes with training wheels.

WE ASKED: How does your preschooler keep entertained?

"Puzzles, books, pretend play with Polly Pocket,
Dora figures, or stuffed animals,
online games, coloring, singing."

—*Stephanie, Hoschton, Georgia*

Will Video Games Melt Your Preschooler's Brain?

EXPERTS SAY YOU should limit your child's "screen time," so you have to wonder if you should even bother to introduce a child as young as three to video and computer games. I've seen grown-ups get hooked on video games, so I can imagine how hard it would be to limit the fun for your preschooler once he's jonesing for another visit to Webkinz or a lap or two around Mario Kart.

The easy solution, of course, would be to put off buying video game consoles, or to hide yours in the closet, and to never show your preschooler that the computer has super fun games to play with SpongeBob while you're busy making dinner.

But if you've got older kids, or you're simply a fan of video games, you might decide to introduce them to your preschooler. Remember, though, that when it comes to young children, not all games are created equal. Here are some tips for picking out appropriate video and computer games for your preschooler:

1. **Violence, even cartoonlike violence, isn't good for your preschooler.** Young kids have difficulties distinguishing between fantasy and reality. All too often, video game violence has no consequences, so your preschooler might think, *Hmmm. If I push my brother off the ride-on toy, he'll magically appear again later. And I'll get extra points!*

2. **Ratings are simply guidelines for you to use to make decisions.** Ultimately, you have to decide which games are

right for your kids. Don't leave that up to the games' manufacturers. Case in point: one video game creator gave a Teen rating to a game called Beer Pong, which means they felt the game was appropriate for pimply faced kids who have algebra homework due tomorrow. Read what other parents write in their game reviews online, such as at Common Sense Media (www.commonsensemedia.org).

3. **Preschoolers lack the fine motor skills to operate certain games.** Many video games have controllers that your preschooler simply isn't developed enough to operate. Chances are, your preschooler won't be able to hold the button down while swinging the controller for Wii tennis, let alone to keep it from ending up wedged into your TV screen. Computer games might be easier for your preschooler to operate.

Once you find games that suit the guidelines you've set for your preschooler, consider these rules for play:

- **Limit game time before you flip the ON switch.** If you leave playtime open-ended, it'll be harder to end it.

- **Make your preschooler work for it.** In other words, make sure he's done his chores, finished eating, and so on before he's given the privilege of playing a game.

- **Play with your preschooler, at least at first.** Maybe you'd rather fold the laundry than travel to Puppyville to meet

Blue's little brother, but if you play video or computer games with your preschooler, you'll get a sense of what she's getting out of it and whether there's anything objectionable in the game.

> ## Okay, I admit it. . . .
>
> "I like being on the receiving end of her make-believe games, such as a customer at her restaurant or a patient at her doctor's office. (That's my favorite. I get to lie down on the couch for five minutes while I get 'examined.')"
>
> —*Elizabeth, Lansing, Michigan*

Does Your Preschooler Need Educational Toys?

WE TWENTY-FIRST CENTURY moms get a little snooty when it comes to toys. If they aren't making our kids smarter or otherwise prepping them for their future at Yale, we tend to think they aren't worth it. We'd much rather hear our preschooler's figuring out patterns on their Leapsters or boning up on phonics on the computer than playing pretend with our shoes and a Star Wars light saber.

Personally, I think it's okay for your preschooler to spend an hour dropping pebbles into a puddle, but I'm a fan of some educational toys, too. My younger son loved his Leapster. He even took it into the bathroom with him, where he'd shout out questions for me through the door. One day, my neighbor, whose kids were too young for educational toys, was in

> ## Okay, I admit it. . . .
>
> "My youngest talks to anything. The other day we caught her talking to the sweeper and carpet cleaners like they were her buddies."
>
> —*Jill, Toledo, Ohio*

my kitchen when he heard something along the lines of, "What's seven plus eight?" He looked around and, bewildered, asked, "Where did that come from?"

But I became used to answering questions while I was on the phone, making dinner, mopping the floor . . . you get the idea. And along the way, I became really good at math. My preschooler became better at it, too, once I made sure he played games that best suited his abilities.

The good news is that there's no shortage of educational games out there for your preschooler, so if you decide to buy a musical toy designed to teach her all about Mozart, you'll be able to find more than one. Just make sure it matches her abilities and attention span, or you'll be answering questions through the bathroom door for quite some time.

WE ASKED: What were your favorite activities to do with your preschooler?

"Having birthday parties for her dolls and Tigger."

—*Roberta, Minneapolis, Minneapolis*

"Believe it or not, we liked cutting and pasting pictures of horses onto a notebook."

—*Jenn, Centerport, New York*

Filling the Hours 'Til Bedtime

TOYS AND GAMES aren't the only way to keep your preschooler entertained. With two preschoolers and many, many long rainy or snowy days at home, I came up with quite a few activities that can keep your preschooler busy (and away from the dog, who just wants to nap). Here are a few of the most popular activities.

Newspaper editor. Fold several pieces of 11" × 17" paper in half and staple them together at the crease. Find some extra photos of your kids, and then ask them to tell you a story about the photo. Write the story on the paper, and then glue the picture next to the story. Or let your preschooler "write" the story by herself.

Clothing sale. Here's a great way to teach your preschooler about money and math. Line up doll clothes and put price tags on each item. Then let your preschooler buy outfits with fake money or real coins, learning what's affordable and what's not. You can do the same thing with action figures, toy cars, LEGOs—anything you've got a lot of around the house.

Treasure hunt puzzles. Hide pieces from a big-piece puzzle throughout the house. Then give your preschooler simple hints for finding them, such as, it's near where daddy lies on weekends while he is watching football. The younger your preschooler, the easier the clues need to be. When he finds all the pieces, help him put it together.

"She plays in her kitchen and serves us. As soon as we pretend to eat the food, she's off again."

—*Shelley, Travis Air Force Base, California*

Gimme a break

Let Your Preschooler Learn to Entertain Himself

Be careful not to turn yourself into your preschooler's personal entertainment director. If he doesn't learn how to play by himself now, it'll be that much harder when he's older. He'll either complain he's bored all day or he'll spend way too much time playing Guitar Hero and not enough time drawing, reading, or playing with friends. Now that your child no longer has to be closely watched every single moment, give him room to play.

Just a minute!

Your Preschooler's Calendar (According to Her)

7 AM: Choose outfit for the day: overalls, tutu, and rain boots, or Easter dress, cowboy hat, and soccer cleats.

7:20 AM   Feed toast crusts to the dog and leftover marmalade to Elmo.

8 AM   Set up tea party as soon as the dog is done licking Elmo's face.

8:30 AM   "Read" plot-less story to Mommy while she pretends to listen over the local news.

9:15 AM   Test rain boots in bathtub (or cleats in pachysandra).

11 AM   Negotiate for prelunch cookies.

12:15 AM   Feed grilled cheese crusts to dog and leftover apple sauce to Elmo.

1 PM   Turn naptime into talk show: interview Winnie the Pooh and forty-seven plastic toy horses. Musical guests: The Wiggles.

2:20 PM   Arrange flowers (across bedroom and under the desk).

2:45 PM   Negotiate for snacks, juice, and another round of Candy Land.

3:15 PM   Change into big brother's baseball uniform, Mommy's high heels, and Burger King crown.

3:30PM   Agree with Mommy to "Thank God for Tivo." Watch a few days worth of Dora the Explorer.

6:15 PM   Present arguments for predinner cookies.

6:30 PM   Feed chicken nuggets to the dog and creamed corn to Elmo.

8 PM   Turn bedtime into talk show featuring the Disney princesses and the game pieces from Monopoly.

Chapter Eight

Why Is the Sky Blue? and *Where Did Grandma Go?*
The Big and Downright Hard-to-Answer Questions

One day after pre-school, my older son asked me why tires are black and how come some dogs have cat ears, triangular ears that perk up rather than the kind that hang down. What am I? Google? The executive producer of Animal Planet?

Preschoolers ask so many questions that, while it's sometimes cute, it can also be downright confounding. They are

Okay, I admit it. . . .

"They begin to ask questions about things that you don't know the answer to yourself, like 'How tall is that oak tree out there?' And 'Why does my fishy stay at the bottom of his fishy home?' They expect you to know the answer to every question that they can come up with."

—*Lisa, Old Town, Florida*

Okay, I admit it. . . .

"I love the silly questions they ask, with all the serious tones in their sweet little voices."

—*Nicole, Howell, New Jersey*

naturally curious, and they think you know everything. And you certainly don't want to prove them wrong.

But what do you really know about why rocks aren't pink or if you can still eat with only half your teeth? And then there are the really tough questions you don't want to flub the answers to, the ones about reproduction and death, for example. How do you handle those?

In this chapter, I'll cover the natural inquisitiveness your preschooler likely possesses. And then I'll offer up ways to handle all sorts of questions.

By the way, the correct answers to my son's questions are:

1. Tires are black because they are made with carbon.

2. Dogs sometimes have cat ears because God made them that way.

Okay, I admit it. . . .

"The worst part about having a preschooler is the constant questions that have no real answers. What are you supposed to say to answer those?"

—*Lisa, Old Town, Florida*

At least, those are the answers I'm sticking with until my grandchildren ask me the same questions.

Because Why?

WHY DOES YOUR preschooler ask "why?" so often? And why does it feel like your head is going to implode like an explosion on *Road Construction Ahead* when you hit your umpteenth "why?" of the day?

Preschoolers are naturally curious, indeed. It's as though they've learned the language, got a chance to look around a bit, and now they've got a ton of questions. And you're the one who's supposed to have the "because" for their "why?" But all that interrogation can get out of hand. Your preschooler asks why you have to pay for your food at the supermarket, and the next thing you know, you're explaining the thought process behind the bar coding system. Hey, at least you're not trying to decipher cries anymore. But you can curb the onslaught of "why?" questions by:

- **Giving honest answers whenever you've got them.** It sounds simple, but if you get frustrated with their questions and start making up answers simply to amuse yourself, your preschooler is going to file them away and come back with other "why?" questions based on wrong answers. And then you'll have to untangle the mess.

- **Holding the sarcasm.** As if a preschooler could understand sarcasm. No, I mean preschoolers don't get sarcasm. Ugh. See what I mean?

- **Asking them what they think.** Preschooler theories are fun to listen to, especially when the question is nearly impossible to answer without the aid of a few MIT graduates or Deepak Chopra.

• **Overfilling your word quota.** If you've got one of those kids who seem to ask "why?" just to ask it, bore her with a long-winded, technical answer, and you just might curb the "why?" questions for a little while.

Here's a secret many parents don't realize: preschoolers often don't want to know why. What? It's true. "Why?" sometimes means, "I think birds are cool. Let's talk about them." But we translate it in our grown-up way. And that's where the trouble begins. Take the following example to see what I mean.

"Why?" the Grown-Up Way

Preschooler: "Why does the cat like to jump up so high?"

You: "Uh, well, cats are natural predators, meaning, they hunt things, like mice. Not that we have mice in the living room or anything. But cats like to get up high so they can survey, er, look around, for things to hunt."

Preschooler: "Kitty is hunting now?"

You: "No, well, Kitty is dozing off. Kitty feels safer being up high."

Preschooler: "Kitty feels safe? From what?"

You: (mumbling to yourself) "The tyranny of grubby little hands."

Preschooler: "Why is Kitty up so high now?"

You: "Because she can."

"Why?" the Preschooler Way

Preschooler: "Why does the cat like to jump up so high?"

You: "Kitty is up high, isn't she? Why do you think she's up so high?"

Preschooler: "Because she's the queen of the kitties."

You: "Oh. And what does the queen do?"

Preschooler: "She is in charge of all the other kitties and the fish and all the grown-ups."

You: "Would you like to be a queen, too?"

Preschooler: "Yes. And then I would be in charge of you and Daddy and the fish, too."

You: "I have to go make dinner."

Preschooler: (ignoring you) "Kitty! You are the queen!"

Kitty: (looking vaguely interested before yawning and going back to sleep.)

See? Sometimes it isn't about the "why?" but about the "what?" She just wanted to talk about cats for a while. So before you get out the encyclopedia or make a trip to PETCO to talk to the folks in charge of cats, find out if your preschooler truly wants to know why, or if she's just in the mood to talk about her favorite things.

WE ASKED: What mind boggling, funny, or difficult questions has your preschooler asked, and how did you answer them?

1. "Where do babies come from?"

   "From an egg in mommy's tummy."

2. "Is Princess Leia real?"

   "No, she's played by an actress called Carrie Fisher."

3. "Can I marry you, Daddy?"

   "No, I'm already married to Mommy."

—*Adam, Allendale, New Jersey*

Where to Find Real Answers

WHEN MY SON was an inquisitive preschooler, I often found myself trying to explain such complex adult topics as how the stock market works, why some animals come from eggs but others don't, and how many violins are in an orchestra. When he asked these kinds of questions—the kind that actually have concrete answers)—I felt compelled to find the answers as best I could. Here are a few of my tricks of the answer trade:

1. **Google it.** It sounds obvious, but if you're not at your computer all day, you might not get a chance to search online that often. You might want to keep a running list of your preschooler's questions, and then search the Net for answers each evening. It'll satiate your preschooler's curiosity while making you feel less like the idiot your kid makes you think you are. Some of my favorite sites to find

answers include AskKids.com and HowStuffWorks.com. Warning: Be careful what you click on when you use search engines. I accidentally clicked through to porn after Googling "cookie." You don't want to know what I found. Trust me.

2. **Keep some go-to folks on speed dial.** My son seemed to ask the most questions while we were out and, therefore, far from the Internet. I liked to share the answering responsibilities with our family, so I called certain people for certain types of answers. For science questions, we tried to stump my sister-in-law, who works in a science lab. For sports and history, we called my mother, who has a knack for remembering all sorts of inane facts and figures. For music recorded before 1960 and money, we called my dad; for music since 1960, my brother; for how things work, my father-in-law or my husband; and for food and anything having to do with Europe, my mother-in-law. They often had to call back with the results, but it got them thinking and amused me greatly to watch them sweat.

3. **Keep a library of topics of interest.** When my son went through his dinosaur phase, we kept books in the house that would answer such questions as "Is T. rex the biggest dinosaur?" Nope, Giganotosaurus. For his killer whale phase, we kept a small library of ocean-related books to answer his questions, like "Are orcas whales or dolphins?" They're dolphins. Not only did it give us the answers, but it

taught him to turn to books for answers, which came in handy when the homework started a few years later.

4. **TiVo topics.** This is the video version of your library of topics of interest. Set your DVR to record all shows about, say, sharks or puppies or whatever your preschooler is into. Weed out the age inappropriate shows, and then see if what's left satiates your preschooler's questions on the topic.

5. **Make an event out of it.** Sometimes a good question can lead to some great afternoon-filling activities, should you find yourself experiencing a particularly long day. If your preschooler asks a question, go find the answer at the library, the pet store, the supermarket, the gas station— wherever you can find the people or the things to help answer your preschooler's question.

Okay, I admit it. . . .

"Maybe other parents google this stuff, but I just make something up."

—*Jenna, Santa Barbara, California*

Answering the Hard Questions

THERE ARE SOME questions your preschooler will likely ask that will make you stumble over the right answer. How do you explain how babies are made? Do you even try? How about why people die? Or why Grandpa had to die? Here are a few of the most common, if not most confounding, questions your preschooler might ask, along with some ways to handle it.

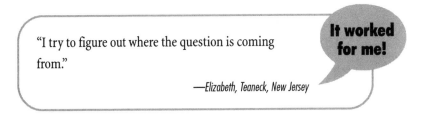

"I try to figure out where the question is coming from."

—Elizabeth, Teaneck, New Jersey

It worked for me!

Question: Why Are Boys Different from Girls?

When my sons were preschoolers, I found them outside my shower between me and my towel. Naturally, they were rather intrigued by what they saw. With no sisters around the house, my boys didn't have many opportunities to discover that girls and boys are built differently. Unfortunately for me, I provided that opportunity in an extremely awkward moment.

If your preschooler is starting to notice that boys' and girls' bodies aren't the same, don't worry. It's part of their normal curiosity. Just hope that they're not noticing it when the lady making bagels for them bends over or a man appears on the beach in a Speedo. Here are some tips for handling questions about body parts and how come yours are different from daddy's:

1. **Keep it simple.** Don't go into long explanations that can confuse or bore your preschooler. Just simply say that boys and girls are made differently and have different private parts.

2. **Think twice about using cute names for sexual organs.** If you decide that jayjay is a great euphemism for vagina, oh

the fun you'll have when she meets a new friend named J.J.

3. **Explain that you use these words with hushed voices.** This will help prevent the embarrassment of an announcement on the playground about your preschooler's penis.

4. **Emphasize the *private*.** Make sure you explain that nobody should touch your preschooler's private parts except the doctor while you're in the room and Mommy or Daddy when they're bathing the kids. Also point out that they shouldn't share their private parts in a public showing, no matter what Britney Spears is doing these days.

Question: Where Do Babies Come From?

Answering this question all depends on your parenting philosophy. If you prefer to say as little as possible when it comes to sex until they're older (like thirty), simply say, "Babies come from Mommy's belly."

But be prepared for the inevitable follow-up question about how the baby got in Mommy's belly. You probably don't want your preschooler to think that you swallowed a baby, so say, "Mommy's egg got fertilized by Daddy's sperm, and they made a baby."

This, of course, can lead to more "how?" questions you might not want to answer. But there are a few things you should consider before you try to skirt the issue:

1. **Don't lie.** Don't make up stories about storks or a baby fairy, because you'll only confuse your preschooler.

2. **Qualify his question.** He might not really want to know exactly how a baby is formed, but rather where he came from—literally. He came from Mommy's belly or, for the scientifically correct among us, Mommy's uterus.

3. **Keep it as simple as possible.** Here's a simple monologue: "A mommy and a daddy who love each other are needed to make a baby. Daddy's sperm (or seed, if you prefer) gets together with Mommy's egg to make a baby, which grows inside Mommy for nine months until it's time to come out."

4. **Don't give misinformation.** If you tell her that kissing is how babies are made, she's going to think she can make a baby if her friend pecks her on the cheek.

 WE ASKED: What's the hardest thing your preschooler has asked you?

"'Am I going to die some day?'
followed immediately by, 'Are *you*?'"

—Jenna, Santa Barbara, California

Question: Why Do People Die?

I'd try to skirt the "why" part, because if you say they get old, it'll be harder to explain why young people die. And if you say people get sick, your preschooler will have a hard time understanding the difference between a head cold and cancer. And not all cancer necessarily kills, so that's hard to explain, too. Here are some tips for explaining death to your preschooler:

1. **Keep it concrete.** Your preschooler views the world in very literal terms. So if you say the dog was "put to sleep," he might think he'll go to sleep at night and never wake up. Instead, explain that somebody's body wasn't working anymore.

2. **Repeat as necessary.** Preschoolers can have a hard time understanding the finality of death. When your preschooler asks if someone who died is coming back, explain calmly but simply that once a person dies, they leave forever. If you believe in the afterlife, explain that they will see so-and-so in heaven when your preschooler goes a long, long time from now.

3. **Be prepared for their responses.** If someone has died, your preschooler may show grief by being clingy or may hide it by pretending nothing is wrong. Or she might be angry. Reassure your preschooler that she didn't cause the death of your loved one, friend, or pet. Let her show her emotions, and don't be afraid to show your grief within reason. You

don't want to scare your preschooler, but you do want to show that it's okay to feel bad when someone dies.

WE ASKED: What's the hardest thing your preschooler has asked you?

"Sophie, age four, asked, 'What's heaven?'
I answered, 'It's where God lives with Grandpa and all the other people who have died.'
Sophie asked, 'God died?'"

—Jenna, Santa Barbara, California

Other Sticky Topics (aka Things You'd Prefer Not to Discuss but Have To)

MY BOYS WERE in preschool when I burst into tears on the phone. I couldn't get a doctor to take my pelvic pain seriously, the function of endometriosis for which I'd ultimately undergo six surgeries. Unfortunately, my preschoolers saw me sobbing. Nicholas, then nearly four, promised he'd help me. If only he had a medical degree.

Sometimes there are very grown-up problems that your preschooler will have questions about. They're too young to truly understand what's going on, but they can sense (or in my case, witness outright) that something's wrong. Here are a few topics with some quick answers. Of course, for very serious or complicated problems, seek out professional help as needed.

Mom or Dad is very sick. As a cancer survivor, I know this is a tough topic to discuss with your kids. But you should tell them

Okay, I admit it. . . .

"Since they are so much more verbal than toddlers, you have to think faster to keep up!"

—*Aubrey, Allegan, Michigan*

you're sick, or they'll fill in the gaps, possibly with something worse. Children often fear that they caused you to be sick or that they can catch your disease. Speak simply but frankly about your illness. Explain that it's not your preschooler's fault and that other people might be helping out while you are in treatment. Encourage them to have fun—that it's still okay to laugh. Some hospitals have family support groups. Or get your preschooler some books to help explain and encourage.

Mom and Dad are getting a divorce. Tell your preschooler only after the decision to divorce has been finalized. Explain that it's not your preschooler's fault, and explain where she will live and when. Reassure her that everything will be fine, only different from what she's used to. Encourage her to talk about it, and be very careful not to blame your spouse or trash-talk him with her. Finally, get some books to help you explain the situation.

Okay, I admit it. . . .

"I know the answers to her questions, but answering them in a way she can understand and not present more questions? That's the trick. I don't want her one question to turn into a string of questions getting more and more complex."

—*Adam, Allendale, New Jersey*

Mom or Dad is remarrying. Preschoolers don't adapt to changes at home that easily, so adding a stepparent and possibly stepsiblings may be hard for yours to understand. Explain in simple terms the new living arrangements, and keep reassuring your preschooler that you love him very much. A good counselor can help your preschooler adjust to the changes at home.

Gimme a break

Put it in Writing.

Keep a book or a blog about the funny, clever, or confounding things your preschooler says. Or add stories to your scrapbooks. My kids love to read about the things they said and thought when they were little, and I love remembering what it was like to feel like their own personal search engine in Keds. If I hadn't written them down, I'd have forgotten half of them.

 **Just a minute!**

To-Do List

1. Buy eggs, flour, bacon, laundry detergent, cereal.

2. Find out how ice cream sprinkles are made and why the Lucky Charms people make the horseshoe marshmallows purple when only unicorns wear purple horseshoes. Duh.

3. Pick up dry cleaning.

4. Google "dry cleaning" to find out exactly how it works. Also, "automatic doors" and "parking meters."

5. Go to the post office.

6. Pick up a copy of *The Post Office Book: Mail and How It Moves.*

7. Pediatrician's appointment, 2:00 PM.

8. Find out how long the average preschooler's tongue is.

9. Make brownies for bake sale.

10. Look up who invented brownies.

Chapter Nine

Taking the "Pre-" off the "K":
Get Ready for Kindergarten

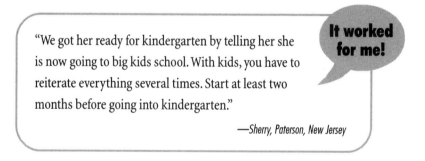

"We got her ready for kindergarten by telling her she is now going to big kids school. With kids, you have to reiterate everything several times. Start at least two months before going into kindergarten."

It worked for me!

—*Sherry, Paterson, New Jersey*

A week before school was to start, I changed my mind. My son had made so many strides in maturity over the summer, I was sure he belonged in kindergarten after all—even though I'd selected our school system's junior kindergarten program, even though his preschool teacher had recommended junior kindergarden, even though he had tested for junior kindergarden.

So for one week, the school's principal humored me by letting my son attend kindergarten. I played it up the best I could, trying to sell kindergarten as the "best ever!" But by Wednesday, he was practically drowning in all the work, and I knew it. I met with the kindergarten teacher who told me what I already knew: my boy wasn't ready for kindergarten. The best thing I could give him was the gift of time.

I put him back in his junior kindergarten class, where he flourished. A year later, he was more than ready to start kindergarten. Every fall since, I find myself very pleased at the decision I made.

Not so long ago, the only thing you needed to prove your readiness for kindergarten was a birth certificate that said you were five year old. But that was before school curricula changed so that the work we used to do in first or second grade is now required in kindergarten. Harder still is the maturity needed to do all that sit-down work. Kindergarten is no longer about play. It's about getting ready for first grade, which is like the third grade of our day.

So how do you get your preschooler ready for the increasingly difficult tasks of kindergarten? More important, can you get him ready?

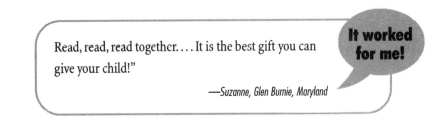

Read, read, read together.... It is the best gift you can give your child!"

—Suzanne, Glen Burnie, Maryland

"To relieve anxiety, we've been talking about how she'll get to ride the bus when she's five years old, and she'll get to go to kindergarten. Not too much about what she'll actually do there, since I don't know yet!

It worked for me!

—*Chrissy, Dillsburg, Pennsylvania*

What Do Kindergarten Teachers Want from Their Students?

BEFORE YOU EMBARK on preparing your child for kindergarten, consider what kindergarten teachers want to see in their students at the beginning of the school year:

1. Good physical health

2. A well-rested child

3. A well-nourished child

Assuming you've got these down, what else do kindergarten teachers want to see? A study by the United States Department of Education found that these were among the most important qualities, in descending order of importance:

• Your child should be able to communicate wants, needs, and thoughts verbally.

• He should exhibit curiosity and enthusiasm toward new activities.

- She should follow instructions.

- He shouldn't disrupt the class.

- She should be sensitive to other kids' feelings.

- He should share.

- She should be able to pay attention.

- He should be able to finish tasks.

Notice it doesn't say anywhere that your child should be able to count to twenty, add, read, play an instrument, do interpretive dances, create a speech about the history of World War II, construct toy giraffes from coffee creamer containers, or type eighty words per minute.

Much of kindergarten readiness has to do with socialization that can't be taught—but it can be fostered. Remember, however, that you can't force maturity. That simply comes with time.

It worked for me!

"To make sure he was socially ready for school, we put him in camps and other social settings where he didn't know very many people; that way he had to make friends."

—*Kristina, Marysville, Ohio*

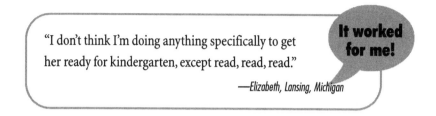

"I don't think I'm doing anything specifically to get her ready for kindergarten, except read, read, read."

—*Elizabeth, Lansing, Michigan*

What Exactly Is Kindergarten Readiness?

THERE'S NO FORMULA to determine whether your preschooler is ready for kindergarten. But there are several main areas of concern, including socialization, motor skills, personal care, language, and basic comprehension skills. Remember, kids at this age change so fast; your child could figure something out in a matter of weeks, even days. Here's what your child's preschool teacher is looking at to assess kindergarten readiness and tips for how to help your child if he is lacking in any of these areas.

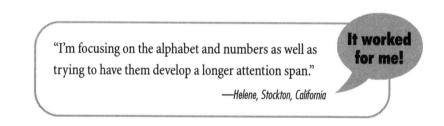

"I'm focusing on the alphabet and numbers as well as trying to have them develop a longer attention span."

—*Helene, Stockton, California*

Socialization

• **Can pay attention for short periods of time.**

Kindergarten prep tip: Assuming that your child doesn't have any serious attention deficit disorders, you can help her improve

Okay, I admit it. . . .

"It wasn't anything I did: She's always been a good listener to her teachers and has a long attention span. I don't think I did anything special. She was just born that way."

—*Michelle, Azusa, California*

her attention span by limiting her television viewing and by reading to her at least fifteen minutes a day. Set up some one-on-one sit down time that you increase slowly as she's better able to sit and listen.

• **Can follow simple directions.**

Kindergarten prep tip: You ask him to bring you a pen, and suddenly, he disappears to go play elsewhere. You can help him learn to follow instructions by giving your preschooler small responsibilities, such as putting away toys or putting his clothes in the hamper. Every time he follows instructions, put a sticker on a chart. When he gets enough stickers, he gets a small reward or privilege. Whenever he doesn't follow instructions, dole out a small consequence, such as less TV time.

• **Can listen to stories without repeatedly interrupting.**

Kindergarten prep tip: Preschoolers pretty much believe the world revolves around them. Also, their short-term memories aren't great, and they tend to be impulsive. And so they interrupt you. Teach her good manners by practicing conversations where she talks, and then you ask, "Are you done speaking?" and vice versa.

• **Is starting to share with others.**

Kindergarten prep tip: Don't expect her to willingly give up her favorite Polly Pocket, but she should be able to share with other kids some of the time. You can help her practice sharing at playdates and with siblings. Just don't push it if she's tired or cranky.

• **Recognizes and obeys authority.**

Kindergarten prep tip: Start to demand respect for adults, and he'll learn who's in charge (and it's not him).

• **Has the beginnings of self-control.**

Kindergarten prep tip: Look, a five-year-old may cry now and then, and that's okay. What they're looking for is that your kid is able to reel it in here and there. It's hard to teach this one, because it's as much about maturity as it is personality.

• **Separates from parents without a major meltdown.**

Kindergarten prep tip: Again, she's *five*. Everyone has a bad day. Some kids have them for the first two months of school. Please give your child a break if she's leaving you teary-eyed for a while. Talk to the teacher if you have concerns.

• **Starts to follow rules.**

Kindergarten prep tip: You have to set rules in order for them to be followed. Make sure you're not teaching him that rules can be broken by letting him get away with breaking them. If you said no feet on the coffee table, then it's no feet on the coffee table—ever. You have to be diligent about enforcing rules in order for your preschooler to learn to follow them.

WE ASKED: How did you get your preschooler ready for kindergarten?

"Lots of play time to develop creativity,
lots of time reading many rhyming and repetition books.
We had some focus at home on learning the letters in their names
and other important words, as well as on social issues like
taking turns or being a good sport during a game."

—*Carissa, Fremont, Nebraska*

"We had a readiness test at his preschool. The things that it said he needed to work on, we did."

—*Monica, Anderson, Indiana*

It worked for me!

Language and Reading

• **Speaks understandably.**

Kindergarten prep tip: If he's got a lisp or other speaking issue, discuss it with the preschool teacher, who can give you some exercises to improve speech. Some kids get speech therapy at school when necessary, but many kids outgrow certain issues before help is needed. Others have hearing problems that affect their speech, so check with your pediatrician if you suspect this might be the problem. Practice is the standard treatment for learning to speak understandably, so have lots of conversations with your preschooler, and correct him as necessary.

• Talks in complete sentences of five to six words or more.

Kindergarten prep tip: Talk, talk, talk and listen, listen, listen. Reading helps, too.

• **Can identify words that rhyme.**

Kindergarten prep tip: Get some books with lots of rhymes in them. Dr. Seuss was a favorite in my house.

• **Identifies some letters.**

Kindergarten prep tip: Please, there's no need to power cram. Your child will learn letters, letters, and more letters in kindergarten. I found that teaching the kids as organically as possible, such as pointing to certain letters when you read to him or asking what letter words like "banana" start with, works best over time.

• **Can start to sound out the beginning of words.**

Kindergarten prep tip: Again, it's about reading. Also, point out letters when you're out and about and remind your preschooler what sound they make. There are video games that can help in this area as well.

• **Can recognize a few sight words, from a list of about two hundred of the most common words in the English language, such as *the*, *not*, and *up*.**

Kindergarten prep tip: Point out a few sight words when you're reading. *Green Eggs and Ham* is a great story to read when you're teaching sight words, because it involves the same fifty words over and over.

Motor Skills

• **Cuts with scissors.**

Kindergarten prep tip: This doesn't mean he should be able to whip up a row of cut-out dolls. It just means he can operate the scissors well enough to cut a paper a few times. Practice with kiddie scissors during arts and crafts time, but don't push it. If your preschooler's fine motor skills aren't advanced enough, he'll get frustrated. You can help work on your preschooler's fine motor skills with Play-Doh or clay.

• **Traces simple shapes like squares and circles (not perfectly, just generally).**

Kindergarten prep tip: Encourage drawing and tracing. Use coloring books, which will help your preschooler practice using a crayon.

• **Can throw and bounce a ball.**

Kindergarten prep tip: Go outside and practice playing with a ball, but remember to make it fun. If it feels like homework, your preschooler likely won't want to do it.

Personal Care

• **Can manage bathroom needs without assistance.**

Kindergarten prep tip: Resist the urge to help your preschooler pull up her pants, button or fasten pants, or wash hands. The more independence you can teach her now, the easier it will be for her in kindergarten.

• Can button and zipper shirts, pants, coats.

Kindergarten prep tip: Please don't expect your kindergartener to button twelve buttons down the front of a shirt or those hard-to-button flies on pants. Keep it simple. You can help his fine motor skills improve with manipulatives, games that require buttoning, zipping, threading laces, putting small toys in holes, and so on.

Okay, I admit it. . . .

"My daughter loves workbooks. She can sit for hours and work to figure out what each page is asking. She'll come looking for help every once in a while, but overall, she is teaching herself through her 'homework,' as she calls it."

—*Jessica, Wichita, Kansas*

WE ASKED: How did you prepare your preschooler for kindergarten?

"Preschool."

—*Katherine, Minneapolis, Minnesota*

Basic Comprehension Skills

• **Understand cause and effect.**

Kindergarten prep tip: Keep a running dialogue whenever your preschooler causes an effect. For example, "See? When you push the door, it closes."

• Understands time of day in a general way (**morning, lunchtime, bedtime, and so on**).

Kindergarten prep tip: Don't expect your preschooler to tell time yet. Instead, ask her questions such as, "When do we have breakfast—morning or night?"

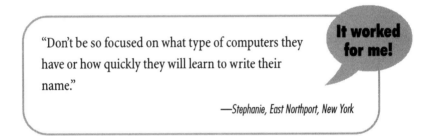

"Don't be so focused on what type of computers they have or how quickly they will learn to write their name."

—*Stephanie, East Northport, New York*

It worked for me!

• **Looks at pictures in a book and then tells a story about them.**

Kindergarten prep tip: Let your preschooler flip through picture books and tell you her own stories.

• **Sorts similar objects by color, shape, and size.**

Kindergarten prep tip: Play with blocks of varying sizes and shape.

• **Can count to ten.**

Kindergarten prep tip: Practice, practice, practice.

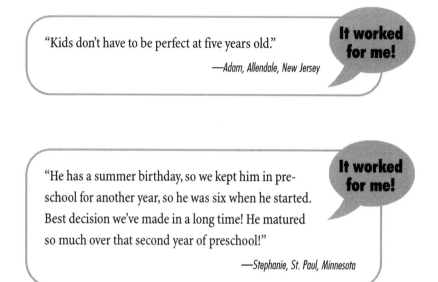

"Kids don't have to be perfect at five years old."

—*Adam, Allendale, New Jersey*

It worked for me!

"He has a summer birthday, so we kept him in pre-school for another year, so he was six when he started. Best decision we've made in a long time! He matured so much over that second year of preschool!"

—*Stephanie, St. Paul, Minnesota*

It worked for me!

That Summer Birthday

IF YOUR CHILD has a summer or early fall birthday that's close to your school system's cutoff date, you might want to consider age when determining kindergarten readiness—but not age alone. A kid born in late August who exhibits many of the signs of readiness listed above will probably do just fine in kindergarten, while a child who shows few signs of readiness may struggle no matter when his birthday is.

Boys, especially, can have difficulties when it comes to summer birthdays and kindergarten readiness. Today's kindergarten is more academically intense than it used to be. Kindergarten teachers have to cram more and more reading, writing, and arithmetic into their days, which are getting longer in many school districts.

Ask yourself if your son (or daughter, for that matter) is ready to sit for long periods, listening, concentrating, and studying. Remember, there isn't as much playtime in kindergarten as we had, and boys especially need to run around a lot.

Note that the number of boys starting kindergarten at age six instead of five has more than doubled in the past three decades. Girls, too, are starting kindergarten older, at nearly double the rate back in the seventies.

Redshirting: It's All About the Game

SOME PARENTS "REDSHIRT," or put off kindergarten a year for their kids simply for the sports benefits. Think about it: if you're a year older than all the other kids, you might also be bigger, faster, better. I guess they're hoping it increases their kids' chances at a college scholarship down the road. But an emotionally ready child shouldn't be redshirted simply because Daddy wants him to have a starting spot on the high school soccer team someday. Rather, a five-year-old who's emotionally and socially ready for kindergarten will get bored with school if he waits a year to start.

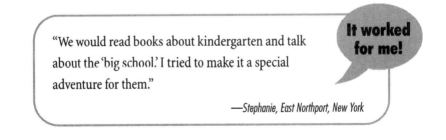

"We would read books about kindergarten and talk about the 'big school.' I tried to make it a special adventure for them."

—Stephanie, East Northport, New York

It worked for me!

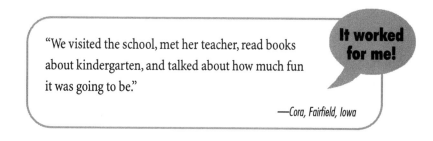

"We visited the school, met her teacher, read books about kindergarten, and talked about how much fun it was going to be."

—Cora, Fairfield, Iowa

Going to the Big Kid School

IF YOU'RE LUCKY, your child's kindergarten will include an orientation session, so your child can visit the school and meet his teacher ahead of time. Our kindergarten even gave the kids a ride around the block in a school bus, which was a very big deal for them. But you don't have to rely on the school to help get your preschooler thinking about kindergarten.

Toward the end of preschool, start talking up kindergarten. If you've got older kids, show your preschooler the kindergarten when you visit the school. In the summer, hang out at the kindergarten's playground, assuming it doesn't interfere with day care or summer camp being held there. Read books about kindergarten, and always make it sound like the most fun place ever.

Before school begins in the fall, treat your preschooler to a trip to the store to buy school supplies, but don't overdo it. If she's got her heart set on a pencil box with unicorns on it, she might be disappointed if the teacher doesn't let her use it. Most teachers send home supply lists, so stick to that. You could explain to your soon-to-be kindergartener that certain school supplies are kept at home, so she can go ahead and get that pencil box. Pick out an outfit to wear on the first day of school, too.

If you can, set up playdates with classmates and kids who will ride on the school bus with your child. It'll help make him less anxious if he sees someone he knows. If there's an older child who can help out on the bus, enlist his help. When my son was in second grade, he spent the first two weeks of school helping two kindergarteners buckle their seat belts on the school bus. He also won the hearts of parents and the school bus driver at the same time.

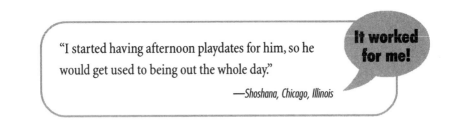

"I started having afternoon playdates for him, so he would get used to being out the whole day."

—*Shoshana, Chicago, Illinois*

It worked for me!

WE ASKED: What's the worst part about having a preschooler?

"Knowing she is going to be going off to kindergarten very soon!"

—*Roberta, Minneapolis, Minnesota*

Gimme a break

Check Out the Kindergarten Yourself

Resist the urge to believe the kindergarten gossip you'll no doubt hear before school begins in the fall. One mother's nightmare teacher might actually turn out to be the best thing for your own kid, while another's favorite might not pan out as well in your family. If a dozen parents are telling you the same thing, then you can probably believe it. Still, how your child does with a particular teacher remains to be seen.

 Just a minute!

Kindergarten Readiness, According to Your Preschooler

- Recites all the names of the dragons and children on *Dragon Tales*.

- Counts through an entire sleeve of thin mint cookies before eating them.

- Draws a decent cat or two—that can fly and talk.

- Spells own name, *mom, dad,* and *cake.*

- Rides a tricycle through the flower beds without getting stuck.

- Fastens own Superman cape.

- Sorts objects in logical categories of toys, snacks, favorite blankies, and stuff to feed the dog when Mommy's not looking.

- Recognizes authority, who happens to wear light-up sneakers.

Chapter Ten

It's Not Just About Me, Me, Me:
Manners, Empathy, and the Environment

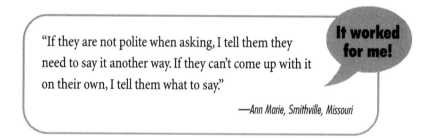

"If they are not polite when asking, I tell them they need to say it another way. If they can't come up with it on their own, I tell them what to say."

It worked for me!

—*Ann Marie, Smithville, Missouri*

My preschoolers were riding quietly in the back of my minivan when I sneezed. Nobody said anything. So I asked, "What do you say when somebody sneezes?" My three-year-old replied, "It's too loud!"

True, but not exactly what I had in mind. What happened to all the manners I had taught them? I had felt like I was telling them a hundred times a day to say "bless you," "please," and "thank you." And yet, here my son had the perfect opportunity to show off his manners, and instead of being the polite boy I had thought I was molding, he sounded more like Spanky on *The Little Rascals*. So I reminded him again what to say when someone sneezes. And it has nothing to do with how loud it was.

Preschool is a key time to really hunker down on teaching kids manners. But it's also a great time to start to instill values in them, including empathy for others and caring for the less fortunate, animals, and the environment. The key is to remember that for preschoolers, the world still revolves around them. Or so they think.

When I was four, everything was "mine." It was such a favored word when I was in preschool that when I turned seventeen, my mother gave me a license plate frame that read "Mine." I remember sitting at a stop light near my high school one afternoon, when I spotted in my rearview mirror two men in the car behind me reading my license plate frame and laughing.

Okay, I admit it. . . .

"When I am on the phone the rule is: You must be bleeding or the house needs to be on fire to interrupt."

—*Bets, Clear Brook, Virginia*

Everybody's been there. The key is to get the "mine" out of your child before it's too late. Repeat, repeat, repeat your manners lessons for your preschooler, and one day, the right answer, to "What do you say when someone sneezes?" just might come from the back of your minivan.

Manners for the "Mine" Age

CHANCES ARE, YOU taught your toddler to say "please" and "thank you," not to mention how to share and why it isn't nice to shut the door in Grandpa's face when he drops by to pick you up for the day. Now that your child is a preschooler, you can raise the bar when it comes to manners.

Perhaps you think your preschooler is too young for civility. After all, he talks to himself —in public—and his best friend is invisible. But manners are part of learning to get along in society in the long run. And now that your child is preschool age, he'll need those skills more and more as he gets out and about with or without you. Manners are a skill, and it's up to you to foster them in him so that he can go off on playdates without getting into a scuffle over every toy or insulting someone else's mom so that she wants nothing to do with your kid.

Okay, I admit it. . . .

"Well, when we are home it's kinda anything goes. It's our only place in the world where we can just be our silly selves. But they still do use please and thank yous when asking for drinks, eats, and so on."

—*Stacy, Monroe, Michigan*

But the acts of good manners, such as opening the door for someone or saying "thank you," are just one part of helping your preschooler learn the ways of the world. When you teach your preschooler good manners, you are instilling good values in him— you know, those part-of-your-soul ideals that mean the difference between appearing on *Cops* as a suspect or as a law enforcement officer. And in an increasingly rude society that's all about "mine," it's a tough job to pull off.

Here are some basic manners that your preschooler should be able to learn, if he hasn't already.

Top Ten Manners for Preschoolers

1. Say "please" and "thank you."

2. Share and take turns.

3. Say "hello" or "hi," working toward looking people in the eye when greeting them. (Obviously shyness plays a role here, so adjust your expectations accordingly.)

4. Use indoor voices—and not just indoors (for example, she doesn't yell, "I gotta go poo!" while on the bleachers at her big sister's softball game).

5. Say "sorry" and after a sneeze "bless you" or "gesundheit."

6. Learn to say "excuse me" properly when interrupting an adult conversation. (In other words, "excuse me" isn't an easy pass into any conversation. You have to wait for permission to speak for it to work correctly.)

7. Don't whisper into someone else's ear in front of other people.

8. Offer help where possible (or impossible—it's still good manners for a forty-pound kid to offer to carry a fifty-pound bag of rock salt across an icy driveway).

9. Knock first.

10. Don't yell from another room or floor in the house.

> "Bend down to his or her level, smile, and say,
> 'Oh sweetie, remember we don't grab or push.
> Let's practice that again.' Not that I've always been so
> calm, but I know I can't teach good manners with yelling—
> which is definitely bad manners."
>
> **It worked for me!**
>
> —*Kristen, Chesapeake, Virginia*

> "Our kids had a nanny from Trinidad for three years
> who spoke in 'please' and 'thank you.' They both say
> 'please' and 'thank you' with authenticity."
>
> **It worked for me!**
>
> —*Arden, New City, New York*

Once More with Feeling

WHEN YOU WITNESS your preschooler pushing another kid out of the way to get to the last cupcake at the birthday party, remember this: manners are not a milestone. They are not a natural progression of development, and so, you must teach them—over and over and over again. Sure, potty training is essentially learned, too. But there's something in it for your child to potty train, including feeling like a big kid, the positive attention, and all that rewards swag. But when your preschooler uses her napkin, what's in it for her?

Eventually, she will learn that it simply feels good to be polite. But that's a long way off. Until then, consider these five guidelines for teaching your preschooler manners so that one day, she'll really say "sorry" with feeling:

1. **Don't be rude.** If you're rude to the salesclerk, the other drivers on the road, or your mother-in-law, you're modeling bad behavior that your preschooler will likely copy. Watch your manners, because your kids are, too.

2. **Repeat, repeat, repeat.** If it feels like you're reminding your preschooler a hundred times a day to say "please" and "thank you," then you're doing a good job of teaching manners. Soon enough, you won't have to remind her of proper manners as much.

3. **Expect respect.** If you let your preschooler treat you like his verbal punching bag, you are teaching him not to respect you. Don't let him interrupt your conversations or get away without apologizing for poor behavior. Expect respect, or you won't get it.

4. **Teach as you go along.** It's easier for your preschooler to understand how you want her to act if you show her how in various social situations. For example, remind her to use her indoor voice as soon as you get to church or synagogue. Or explain that she should put her napkin in her lap when you sit down for dinner at her grandparents' house.

5. **Use rewards and consequences.** If your preschooler helps his little brother get off a chair, stop and point out how

proud you are of him. If he continues showing manners, reward him with a small treat, such as more TV time or an afternoon with just Mommy. If he misbehaves, though, use a punishment that fits the crime.

Say You're Sorry, Even If You're Not?

Remember these two words: "I apologize." They're a great substitution for "I'm sorry," which no preschooler (or adult, really) wants to have to say when he doesn't mean it. "I apologize" doesn't necessarily require you to actually feel sorry. And, chances are, your preschooler doesn't, anyhow.

Practice with your preschooler, so she knows how to say it, so it doesn't sound like she's being held captive and forced to say things she doesn't mean. And—this is extremely important—apologize to her when applicable. Also, apologize to your spouse and others in front of your preschooler. Not only will she learn how it's done, you just might become a kinder, gentler family.

"Speak to your children the way you would like to be spoken to. Lead by example."

It worked for me!

—*Bets, Clear Brook, Virginia*

WE ASKED: Do you think today's kids are more or less well mannered than previous generations and why?

"There is a sense of entitlement among people. They don't need to be polite, and they have a me, me, me attitude. If parents act that way, their children will too."

—*Melissa, Salt Lake City, Utah*

Monkey See, Monkey Do

SOMETHING HAPPENED AFTER *The Cosby Show* left TV: rudeness started seeping into our television programming. From the Rugrats' obnoxious behavior to reality show misdeeds, manners have left the airwaves in droves. And when your kids see rude behavior on TV, they think it's okay to behave that way in person.

Be diligent not only about filtering out violence and sex from your preschooler's TV and movie viewing, but also rudeness. Don't assume that a G-rated TV show is void of objectionable material. Even Tom and Jerry are rude if you think about it. Not that I think cartoons will teach your children to drop anvils on other people. But if everything they see on TV has an undertone of rudeness, they're more likely to pick up that behavior and try it themselves.

If your preschooler witnesses rudeness on TV, use the opportunity to explain why it's wrong to be as rude as SpongeBob is to Squidward and vice versa. Or why we don't behave like the pushy paparazzi on *Access Hollywood* and why it's not okay to talk like a guest on *Dr. Phil*.

And don't think your preschooler isn't paying attention to the TV that's on while they're doing something else. They're picking up words, sights, and behaviors just by playing nearby, so don't keep the TV on as background noise, and flip the channel if something objectionable comes on. I always keep my finger on the jump button of the remote, just in case my kids walk in while I'm watching grown-up shows.

Make your TV model good manners just like you do . . . you do, right?

 WE ASKED: What kinds of good manners do you expect from your preschooler?

"Modesty, especially with the girls—no flipping up the dress to show the diaper or underwear!"

—*Ann Marie, Smithville, Missouri*

"*Asking* for a desired item as opposed to demanding."

—*Heidi, Charleston, West Virginia*

Manners 101

WHILE TEACHING YOUR preschooler to say "please" and "thank you" are most likely part of your everyday teachable moments, other manners take a little more planning to get across. The key is to take one or two goals and work toward those until you feel your preschooler is ready to step it up a notch. Here's the how-to on some basic manners your preschooler may well be ready to learn.

How to Behave in Public

Your preschooler has a busier social calendar now, visiting friends for playdates and playing on playgrounds. Plus, people

> **It worked for me!**
>
> "I will gently remind my daughter when she slips with her manners. I also explain the behavior I expect when we are going somewhere."
>
> —*Bets, Clear Brook, Virginia*

expect better behavior from your preschooler now that she's beyond the toddling-through-Target stage. It's time to expect more, too.

For instance, before you enter a store, remind your preschooler to use her indoor voice; walk, don't run; and stay by your side. When she suddenly dashes off because she's excited to rummage through the hot pink backpacks—do not yell across the store. Remember? You told her to use her indoor voice, so why aren't you? Instead, catch up to her, get down to her level, turn her toward you, and calmly remind her not to run off from you.

This isn't the time to carry on about how she doesn't listen and then complain to the other mothers passing by about your preschooler's inability to follow instructions. She's still learning manners. And there were backpacks with Cinderella on them! No wonder she ran off.

Continue to remind her of the rules, even if it makes you feel like you're saying "Don't run!" so often that the clerks at the supermarket are even tired of it. But the clerks aren't responsible for raising your preschooler right. You are. You need to repeat yourself a lot when you teach manners. Those clerks will appreciate your efforts when your preschooler no longer whines for gum or dashes off to the ice cream aisle when you're not looking.

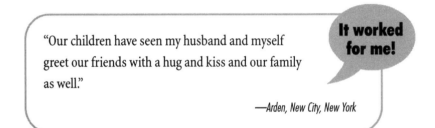

"Our children have seen my husband and myself greet our friends with a hug and kiss and our family as well."

—Arden, New City, New York

It worked for me!

How to Greet People

Minimally, your preschooler can learn to say "Hi" when Daddy walks in from a business trip, rather than, "What did you bring me?" Simply acknowledging someone's presence is a doable feat for most preschoolers no matter who just walked in the door. But imploring, "Say hello, Tyler," while your preschooler is busy drawing isn't enough to teach him how to meet and greet. Rather, you need to treat greetings like you're in the Blue Room at the White House where the president traditionally receives guests. In other words, make a more formal effort of it.

When visitors arrive at your house, make sure your preschooler is by your side. Don't bill it as the boring "how ya doing?" that it might seem to your preschooler. Rather, give him the job of opening the door. Preschoolers love grown-up responsibilities. And, chances are, you've taught him never to open the door unless you say so, so he thinks of it as a treat.

Then, make a point to introduce your preschooler to your visitors, even the adults. Don't expect him to do much more than say "Hi" at this point. If you've got a social kid, encourage him to shake hands and look the visitor in the eye. But if your child is shy, don't force it. Even grown-ups have a hard time with that.

Okay, I admit it. . . .

"I try to get them to look at an adult when they are talking to them. (It is really hard though!)"

—*Kris, Clarkfield, Minnesota*

When you'll be the visitors, tell your preschooler he must first say "hi" before he's allowed to enter the house. Don't let him run off with a friend until he has sufficiently greeted the person or people in the front hall.

When you run into friends or family while you're out, be careful not to get caught up in conversation about, say, back-to-school night until you've all said your hellos all around. If you continue to make a big deal about greetings, it will soon become a natural reaction for your preschooler.

How to Get Along with Friends

Preschool is all about socialization, so your child will learn a lot about getting along with others at school. But you can certainly reinforce the preschool's teachings at home. There are three basics of getting along with others that you can concentrate on with your preschooler.

Sharing. This isn't just about breaking up a fight over a toy. It's about teaching your preschooler to offer her friend a cookie when she's having one or to give a friend a toy to play with on playdates.

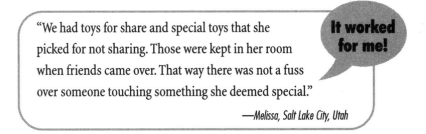

"We had toys for share and special toys that she picked for not sharing. Those were kept in her room when friends came over. That way there was not a fuss over someone touching something she deemed special."

—*Melissa, Salt Lake City, Utah*

It worked for me!

It's about going from a defensive to an offensive approach. You're working from, "Now, now, Brandi, let Sophie play with the dollhouse, too," toward, "That was nice of you to let Sophie play with the jump rope first, Brandi." You teach her how to share through positive reinforcement and gentle encouragement.

Hosting. This is a hard one for your preschooler to learn, because he doesn't understand what makes his pal Mike so special simply because he's at your house now. But it's reasonable to expect your preschooler to learn to be a good host. Show him by serving snacks and meals to his guest first. Teach him by reminding him to ask his friend if he'd like a drink, or by making sure he lets his friend walk up the stairs first.

Helping. When you pick up your preschooler from a playdate, ask her to help clean up the toys before she leaves—even if the other mom says she doesn't have to. (Just explain you're teaching manners and that you expect your daughter to help clean up.) If your preschooler's playdate is having trouble figuring out how to set up the tee for T-ball, encourage your child to help her. At this age, helping others makes them feel grown-up, so use that to your advantage when you're teaching your preschooler manners.

> **It worked for me!**
>
> "Try to explain before the playdate that she needs to share and use manners. Give examples: Sabrina might want to play with your doll. See if you can trade with her if that happens or take turns."
>
> —*Kristen, Chesapeake, Virginia*

> **It worked for me!**
>
> "We are working on the concept of kindness. It is kind to play nicely with the things that we have; to be kind to our dog, no tail pulling; and so on."
>
> —*Heidi, Charleston, West Virginia*

How to Behave at the Dinner Table

Now that your preschooler can use a fork and can get in and out of her chair on her own, it's time to introduce more advanced table manners. There's a lot for her to learn, so don't try to load it on her all at once. Rather, start small. Work on one or two of these important parts of good table manners at a time:

- Washing hands before eating
- Holding utensils properly
- Using a napkin (instead of sleeves) and keeping it in her lap (instead of on the floor)
- Eating with her mouth closed
- Asking for, rather than demanding, food to be passed
- Saying "please" and "thank you"
- Clearing plates from the table (unless you're using your good china and she's clumsy)
- Saying "excuse me," instead of disappearing mid-potato, and waiting to be excused

Don't just expect table manners at home. Reinforce them at other people's houses, as well.

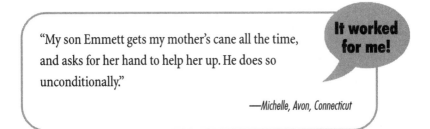

"My son Emmett gets my mother's cane all the time, and asks for her hand to help her up. He does so unconditionally."

—Michelle, Avon, Connecticut

It worked for me!

Do Unto Others

YOU CAN TALK about the poor children elsewhere in the world all you want, but it's hard for your average preschooler to grasp what that has to do with him. I have found that it's best to teach your children compassion and regard for less fortunate people in more tangible ways. Here are a few ways that I taught my preschoolers to care for the sick and the poor.

Give it away. A month or so before Christmas, I present my kids with empty boxes and ask them to put toys that they no longer play with in them, in part to make way for Santa's upcoming delivery, but also to give less fortunate kids toys. I make sure they don't fill the boxes with broken or otherwise useless stuff. And I have them help me deliver it to the church or elsewhere, so they can be

Gimme a break

Don't Let Your Preschooler Get Away with It

Don't fall prey to the "they're only little once" mentality that has become more prevalent in recent years. While your preschooler might not have the patience to sit quietly through your hour-long eye doctor appointment, don't give her a free pass to act like an MTV reality show contestant wherever you go: loud and rude. If you're constantly embarrassed by your preschooler's behavior wherever you go, start working on changing it, one "please" and "thank you" at a time. It takes work, but remember that it's easier to teach a four-year-old to treat you and others with respect than it is a twelve-year-old who's gotten away with behaving badly for her entire life.

a part of helping other people beyond the room clearing. Also, our kids give a dollar of their own money to the church collection on Sundays, and they help me gather school supplies, food, and other items for various charity collections.

Point it out. If we spot a homeless person or a person in a wheelchair, I discreetly explain how fortunate we are to have a home and health. I use (carefully screened) examples in the newspaper and on the news. And I praise my children whenever they make the extra effort to help someone who's not as strong as they are, from a younger neighbor to a pet to the elderly.

Give them a job. I teach responsibility to my kids by assigning

"After a recent hospital stay, we talked about the other children that he saw at the hospital and then gathered some of his outgrown toys and took them to the pediatric unit playroom."

—Heidi, Charleston, West Virginia

It worked for me!

"My three-year-old loves the dog, so she has appointed herself 'Feeder of the Dog.' It's something that she enjoys doing, and it makes her feel like she is contributing to the family. I try to praise her when she does a good job. That makes her beam, and she will turn around and say, 'Thanks Mom!' with the sweetest smile on her face."

—Susan, La Fayette, Georgia

It worked for me!

them jobs. My younger son is in charge of feeding the fish in his room. When he was younger, we supervised the feedings so the fish wouldn't wind up swimming in half a bottle of fish food. When my neighbors go away, I make sure my kids help me take care of their cat. There's nothing like a little poop scooping to teach your kids to care for pets.

Be on the lookout. I teach my kids to keep an eye out for someone who might need help. Whether it's an elderly person who needs help opening the door at a store or me, arms full of grocery bags, they've learned to look for someone to help. Much of the time, I no longer have to remind them. But it took constant reminders from their preschool days and beyond to get to this point, so don't give up!

Just a minute!

Between the Lines:
A Formal Invitation

You are cordially invited to a tea party

*during which you will get your butt stuck in
a kid-sized chair*

in the playroom

*behind the giant pile of LEGOs, but in front
of the dress-up clothes*

at four o'clock this afternoon

*right around when it becomes clear that someone
isn't ready to give up her nap.*

Black tie.

*Also, red, paisley, striped, full of little Santas,
and others found in Daddy's closet.*

R.S.V.P. by snack time.

Or the bears get your share.

Chapter Eleven

You're a Big Girl Now
(So Go Clean Your Room):
Fostering Your Preschooler's Independence

She was only four, and yet she was helping her mom. My friend's daughter picked up her plate and brought it into the kitchen where she deposited it, just like her mother had told her to. Meanwhile, my boys had disappeared.

Well, I told myself, *she's got four kids, so she has to train them better than I do.* But then I realized that if her four-year-old could do what she'd asked, my four-year-old could do the same.

Um, she's a girl, and girls are more mature than boys, I consoled myself. But they all have two hands—and dirty plates—I remembered.

She's a better mother than I am? I panicked. At the very least, her kids are more independent, I decided. And so I set out to stop being my preschoolers' waitstaff and start teaching them some independence. And frankly, it took a while. Part of the problem was me: I just had to get over taking care of anything and everything for my preschoolers.

The sooner you teach your children to take care of themselves, the better off they'll be when school responsibilities and activity schedules start to weigh heavily on them. I don't mean that you should hand your three-year-old a shovel and show him to the mulch pile. That's a sure way to end up with mulch all over your deck. Rather, I mean that you have to start giving your kids age- and temperament-appropriate responsibilities—even if none of the other kids in the neighborhood have to do such things.

As your child reaches kindergarten age, it's a great time to add on small but worthwhile duties. Your preschooler will likely want to act like a big kid, and she's still young enough to like helping out Mommy. Plus, the older your kids are when you start instilling independence and responsibility, the more likely they are to look at you as though their personal maid has gone crazy. Don't let that happen! Start now.

> **It worked for me!**
>
> "Preschoolers can do so much more than toddlers, and they love showing off their newfound skills. Instead of having to stop what I'm doing to make sure my toddler is not getting into trouble, I have my preschooler right by my side, working with me."
>
> —Elizabeth, Lansing, Michigan

What Can Your Preschooler Do?

YOUR PRESCHOOLER WILL need a certain amount of independence to make it in kindergarten. Teaching him a little independence now will help him when, say, it's time to go outside to the playground, and he doesn't need help getting his jacket zipped. He's learned some of these things in preschool, but now it's time to step it up for the big kid school. But how can you help him get ready for independence? Here are a few tips:

1. **Make it easy.** Give your preschooler simple tasks she can complete without getting frustrated. Ask her to pull on a shirt over her head, rather than giving her a button-down shirt. Or let her pour her own milk from a small container, rather than asking her to hike up a gallon jug or a bulky half-gallon carton that has no handle.

2. **Tell him how to do it in easy steps.** If you stand him in front of a floor full of toys and clothes and say, "Clean this up," he will likely feel overwhelmed and wind up sitting in the middle of the mess, playing. Instead, give him step-by-step instructions, such as, "Put those three toys in the toy box. Good! Now put your socks in the hamper." Breaking down the tasks makes it easier for him to handle.

3. **Set a deadline.** Tell your preschooler she will clean up her floor until the "big hand on the clock hits the six." Better yet, use an egg timer so your preschooler, who probably

can't tell time yet, can watch the time tick down while
she works.

4. **Praise, praise, and praise some more.** The more positive
feedback he gets, the more likely he'll try it out again.
I mean, who wouldn't want a pat on the back for
cleaning up?

 WE ASKED: What kinds of responsibilities have you given your
preschooler?

"Putting dirty clothes in his hamper in his room.
Putting away toys. Throwing his empty snack wrappers
in the garbage. Putting his shoes where
they go when we take them off."

—*Kristy, Greenville, Pennsylvania*

Not So Fast . . .

PART OF TEACHING your preschooler to be independent has to do
more with you than with him. When your preschooler struggles
with something new, how fast do you jump in to help? If you're
always standing by like a roadie at
a Bruce Springsteen concert,
ready to pick up something he
drops or help him get off the
playground slide, you're teaching him to rely on you for way
too much.

Okay, I admit it. . . .

"He is more independent, but
he still wants me to do things
for him."

—*Kristina, Marysville, Ohio*

As he gets older, learn to back off more and more. Of course, if it looks like he's about to clock himself or fall, jump in and thwart the boo-boo. But if you're not in a rush to get somewhere, let him try to manage more things on his own.

Here are some age appropriate examples of fostering greater independence.

The self-care hop. It's very clear that your preschooler is having a heck of a time getting her shoes on. You want to race over and rescue her from her fussing and fidgeting. But she's not getting overly frustrated, and you're in no rush to go anywhere. What should you do?

Nothing. Just watch from afar while she works at it some more. If she's clearly doing something wrong, like putting the left shoe on her right foot or trying to cram her foot into her little sister's too-small shoe, let her know. Otherwise, let her try to get her shoe on. If she asks for help, loosen the laces a bit and let her try again. But if she's on the verge of tears, help out. You don't want her to get so frustrated that she gives up altogether.

The dinnertime jumble. Your preschooler is trying to spoon peas onto his plate. Steady, steady, steady . . . try to breathe, Mom. What's the worst that can happen? He can spill the peas. What should you do?

Let him try, even if it means you're going to wind up with peas all over the table. Now, if he's balancing those peas over the gravy boat, move the gravy. And if he's about to dump buttery peas all over Grandma's homemade tablecloth that you only take out on Thanksgiving, maybe now's an okay time to help him balance that spoon. But if you do, don't take it away from him, just offer a little help, and then praise him for successfully getting those peas to his plate.

The playground endeavor. Your preschooler is contemplating getting on a playground toy he's never tried before. All of his friends have climbed up on the age-appropriate apparatus, but he's standing there, staring. You can tell he wants to get on it, but isn't sure if he can. What should you do?

Don't move. Don't say a word. Pretend to be busy talking to other parents when he looks your way. Let him give it a try on his own, and if he needs help getting on it, or if it looks like he's about to fall headfirst, offer your assistance. Part of learning is trying, and the playground is a great place for your preschooler to gain some confidence.

The car dismount. Your preschooler is waiting for you to help her out of the car, just like you always have. But now you've got a baby and some bags to lug, so it'd be a great time for your thirty-plus-pound kid to get herself in and out of the car. What should you do?

If you've got a big SUV without door runners, keep a milk crate in the car that your preschooler can step on to get in and out of the car. Otherwise, she should be able to climb in and out on her own with your light supervision (standing nearby, especially in a parking lot, holding the door open, but not hiking her into the car). You can also teach her to put on her own seat belt, unless it's one of those complicated car-seat buckles with multiple clasps, in which case, you should still be in charge.

The precarious carry. Your preschooler has decided to help you clean up the living room, which was great until he picked up the expensive vase you got as a wedding gift. What should you do?

Don't flip out! If you do, you'll scare him, which may make him drop it. Instead, tell him the vase is for grown-ups only to carry, and then point out which things would be best for him to help clean up. Make sure you praise him a lot so that he wants to help you out again.

The mother's helper. Your preschooler has decided that she's the big sister and, therefore, should help you take care of the baby. But her idea of helping you is to shove a pacifier in the baby's mouth when the baby clearly doesn't want it. What should you do?

Give her set responsibilities that pretty much keep her away from the baby. Send her to fetch a spoon, baby powder, a blanket, and so on. Make it her job to refill the diaper holder when it starts to get low or to put the baby's socks away. That way, she'll feel like she's in charge, while keeping her from potentially harming or just plain annoying the baby.

The little errand runner. You're in Walmart, and your preschooler wants to help you. You're tired, and you just want to get out of the store and go home. But he's busy "helping" you pick up a jumbo package of toilet paper, which he's managed to get off the shelf but is struggling to hoist up. He looks like an Olympic weight lifter who's about to reach his limit. What should you do?

Say "thank you" and help him put it in the cart. Then say, "Hey, can you go grab some of those napkins for me, buddy?" He'll forget all about the oversized toilet paper package because now he's a man on a mission for napkins. Keep it up throughout the store, avoiding the glass containers, eggs, or other jumbo packaging, and you'll help foster independence while getting the shopping done so you can go home.

> **It worked for me!**
>
> "Preschoolers are also able to do a bunch on their own. They learn to buckle their own seat belt! They move from sippy cups and diaper bags to water bottles and backpacks full of toys."
>
> —*Shelley, Travis Air Force Base, California*

When You Don't Have to Foster Independence

Today's moms feel a lot of pressure to be perfect all of the time. So if we don't take that chance to teach our kids to be independent like the parenting magazines and the books say we should, we feel guilty. We wasted a teachable moment! Oh, the horror!

Okay, I admit it. . . .

"Preschoolers are convinced they can do it all by themselves, which makes getting things done a lot more time consuming"

—*Ronique, Urbana, Illinois*

You know what? Sometimes you have to cut yourself some slack. Sometimes you have to scoop the peas for your preschooler or pick up that toilet paper at the store and not turn your shopping trip into a life lesson for your kid. And that's okay.

WE ASKED: What's the worst part about parenting a preschooler?

"That heartache that your baby is not a baby anymore. They are growing up way too fast. All I can say is it really seems to have gone fast when you look back, but in the moment of stress you say, 'Gosh, I will be so happy when they can . . .'"

—*Sachia, Independence, Missouri*

Gimme a break

Remember, You Make the Rules

You're trying to teach your preschooler some independence, but your mother keeps undermining your efforts. She doesn't think "the baby" should have to put on his own coat yet, not when Grandma is there to "helpy welpy." Barf! If your mother won't get on board with fostering your preschooler's independence at her house, make house rules she must abide by when she visits.

If you're under the weather, cranky, tired, worried about paying the mortgage, PMSing, sleep deprived, or just plain not in the mood to better your preschooler's life at this moment, that's okay. Just don't be snippy about it with your preschooler. Quietly guide that spoonful of peas or grab that toilet paper, and don't make a big deal about it. You'll have plenty of chances to foster independence later.

Boost Confidence with Special Tricks

Well, not a magic trick or a circus act, but if you can give your preschooler one thing she can do that many of the other kids can't, you'll boost her self-confidence greatly, thereby encouraging her to be more independent overall. But what can you teach her? It all depends on her abilities, interests, and attention span. If, for example, she shows an interest in learning to tie her shoes and has the fine motor skills and patience to give it a go, teach her how.

I'm not suggesting that you spend hours each night trying to give your preschooler an edge over the other kids. I'm just saying that your preschooler might have some natural abilities that you can foster now. The real trick is figuring out what those abilities are and then encouraging them without intensity. Here are a few kindergarten- (or older) level activities that you might be able to teach your preschooler now:

• Reading	• Playing sports
• Tying shoes	• Playing music
• Writing	• Riding a bicycle

WE ASKED: What do you wish someone had told you about parenting a preschooler before your child entered that stage?

"Don't take things personally when they are trying to gain their independence."

—*Suzanne, Glen Burnie, Maryland*

Chores for Your Preschooler

NOW THAT YOUR preschooler has the gifts of language, fine motor skills, and some semblance of reason, you can assign him age-appropriate chores. But before you hand him the mop, consider what may and may not work at this age. Here are some chores you can reasonably expect your preschooler to perform:

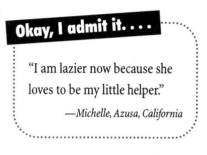

Okay, I admit it. . . .

"I am lazier now because she loves to be my little helper."

—*Michelle, Azusa, California*

- Simple food prep, such as helping you get food out of the fridge, putting things in a pot (supervised!), and so on

- Setting the table

- Clearing plates from the table (but not sharp knives or easy-to-spill stuff)

- Washing and drying plastic dishes

- Dusting

- Emptying garbage cans (with assistance)

- Folding towels, matching socks, putting folded clothes in drawers

- Cleaning up spills (especially their own)

- Putting away toys

- Putting clothes in the hamper

- Straightening up

- Helping feed pets

- Mopping (with help)

- Carrying small bags in from the car

How to Be the Chore Master

One of the best things about preschoolers is that they love to imitate Mom and Dad. Use that to your advantage by letting them help you do chores. If, for instance, you're dusting, give your preschooler his own duster to help you out. Sounds simple, right?

Ah, but there's more to it than that. Here's what you need to keep in mind if you're in charge of doling out the chores to your preschooler:

1. **Don't expect your preschooler to perform chores perfectly.** If, for example, you've asked your preschooler to hang up the towels in the bathroom, don't call her back in to show her what a half-baked job she did. This isn't the Hilton. Your preschooler is too young to hang up the towels the nicely neat way you'd do it. And don't tell her she did a great job when the bathroom looks like the high school's boy's locker room after the big game. Praise her for her efforts and move on.

2. **Don't nag.** I mean, who wants to help a nag? Instead, set up a chart of responsibilities for your preschooler and

everyone in the house (except the baby, of course). Set up time each day for everyone to get chores done, and your preschooler will begin to see it simply as a part of his daily schedule. Soon, he will see that he's an important part of running the house.

3. **Make it fun.** You don't have to create a puppet show out of the socks in the laundry pile to make it fun for your preschooler. But if chores are, well, a chore, it's going to be hard to keep your preschooler's interest. Soon you'll give up getting her to help out, and before you know it, you're vacuuming under your tween's feet, while she text messages her pals about how you're making it impossible for her to hear the TV. It doesn't take much to make chores fun for your preschooler:

   - Ask her to find out who can pick up the most toys before your egg timer goes off in thirty seconds.
   - See how many "shots" she can make into the washer with her clothes.
   - Give her a handheld vacuum and let her go at the couch cushions. (Tip: First remove large items like pencils and coins that will kill the mini-vac.)
   - See who can sweep up the most stuff in the house, with extra points for the most eclectic collection of stuff. ("Look! A hair tie, a quarter, a golf pencil, and a plastic hula dancer!")

Enlist Help in Planning

Ask your preschooler what kind of chores he can help you do. If you give him the choice of responsibilities, he's more likely to "own them," taking pride in getting them done. Also, he probably won't whine when it's time to do his chores. You might want to have him help you design a chore chart, which can be a graph where you mark completed tasks with stickers or stamps. Or it can be a wheel chart, where your kids take turns completing various chores. Just make sure they're age appropriate, so you don't set up your little ones for failure, frustration, and then, possibly, rebellion.

Pick out the rewards ahead of time. Whether you hand out an allowance, reward with desserts or other goodies, or offer up privileges in exchange for chores is up to you. But make sure you offer up the reward ahead of time, so your preschooler knows what she's working toward. Some parents, however, don't believe in a reward system for chores. They believe that everyone in the family has to chip in pretty much for the privilege of living in the house. Figure out your chore philosophy before you embark on doling out the chores, so there's no confusion.

Follow through with consequences. Your preschooler will better understand that chores are a necessary part of the household activities if there are consequences for not following through. If, for instance, she refuses to clean up her toys, she loses the privilege of watching her favorite TV show. Be consistent, or your preschooler will remember that one time you let her watch *Caillou* slack-jawed while you cleaned up for her, and she'll go for it again.

WE ASKED: What's the best part about parenting a pre-schooler?

"Being able to include them in just about any activity, from fun outings to chores at home."

—*Katherine, Minneapolis, Minnesota*

"The independence. Hee."

—*Jen, Fort Thomas, Kentucky*

When Preschoolers Shun Independence

ALL OF A SUDDEN, your oh-so-helpful preschooler is boycotting you and your plans to make him more independent. While he used to cheerfully help you pick up the toys, now he's hiding behind the kitchen table in protest while you try to coax him out with bribes, threats, anything to get your preschooler back on track. What's up with him, and why doesn't he want to be independent anymore? There are a few things that could be going on.

There's a new baby in the house. And that baby doesn't have to put away her shoes, so why, thinks your preschooler, should he? He protests all the attention that the baby is getting by refusing to try to be a big kid. And one way to do that is to act like a little kid— a little kid who is now having an all-out meltdown over a couple of toys you just asked him to pick up. What should you do?

He thinks that if he acts like a baby, he'll get the same kind of attention the baby's getting from all those visitors carrying presents in baby-style wrapping paper. Tell him that you know it can be hard to be the big brother. Offer him some big kid time—time when you do something with him that the baby can't do, like play a game or watch a favorite TV show together. Dole out hugs and kisses; rebill chores as the fun, just-for-big-kids activity you'd like him to believe they are.

She's afraid she's going to do something wrong. First, ask yourself if she got the idea that she's bad at chores from you. Did you criticize her work? Rush in and fix everything she did? Yell at her? Or maybe she failed at something else, and she's fearful it'll spill over into her chores. What should you do?

Boost her self-confidence by overpraising her a bit until she gets back in the swing of her chores. Did she dust the lamp? Tell her you're so glad she did that, because you were worried that it would stay dusty. Did she put away the toys that her playdate had strewn about? Thank her for helping you out. The more she sees how well she's doing, the more her confidence will be restored.

He's scared you'll stop taking care of him. The preschool years are marked by numerous advances that can scare a kid. To him, it seems like just yesterday that you changed his diapers and filled his sippy cup for him. (Maybe it was just yesterday.) The more responsibilities he has, the more he feels like he's losing you. What should you do?

Everybody needs a little TLC now and then. Make sure you still help when he really needs it. And snuggle, cuddle, and hug him often. Soon enough, he won't want you to. And then you'll need TLC!

Just a minute!

The Preschool Palace:
A Five-Star Hotel

Here at the Preschool Palace, you will be wrapped in luxury.

We believe that you deserve the very best—also, that you need not lift a finger.

We do it all for you!

Need the toy you dropped?

Don't worry; our attentive bellhop service will take care of it for you.

Don't feel like getting up to join the family at the dinner table?

We will serve it to you on the coffee table while you watch yet another episode of *SpongeBob SquarePants*.

Would you rather stay home from school today?

Sure! We'll even entertain you with board games and a marathon session of Super Mario Brothers—deluxe edition, of course.

Tired of zipping your coat, putting your shoes away, and brushing your teeth?

We have assistants to take care of that for you.

Whatever your needs, we will tend to them, so you don't have to.

Enjoy your stay!

Chapter Twelve

Me, Myself, and I:
You Minus the Mom Bits

 WE ASKED: How did you spend the hours your child was in preschool?

"Worrying about her!"

—*Cora, Fairfield, Iowa*

I was a mom on a mission. I wanted to find enough black felt to fill our front windows with a whimsical Halloween decoration involving cut-out ghost faces I'd seen in *Parents* magazine. Only, I don't like whimsy. And I'm not all that crafty, either.

I dropped off my firstborn at preschool and carted my toddler to the local craft shop where, I soon found out, they don't carry swaths of felt that big. Rather, I would have to go to a special felt

187

broker who could custom cut the felt for me. By the time I found the store, hidden in an industrial area two towns away, it was nearly time for pickup at the preschool. As the felt cutter made small talk, I checked my watch and plied my two-year-old with crackers. When the guy finally finished cutting my felt, I rushed out of the building, strapped my son into his car seat, and raced over to the preschool just in time.

Two days later, when my son was in preschool again, I got out my felt, drew funny faces in metallic pen, cut them out and taped white tracing paper behind them. Then I tacked them up in the front windows. That night, I turned on the lights. My ghost windows were a big hit—and they still are, every October.

But they were also a sign that I needed to be creative again. I'd spent much of the previous three-plus years pretty much undoing everything my kids did, changing diapers, cleaning up messes, disarming chubby hands wielding crayons too close to the wall. It was time for me to, well, be me again. So I started writing. By the time my second son was in preschool, I launched MommaSaid.net, and in time, I created a work-at-home career that keeps me out of the felt factories.

Whether you've been home with the kids for a while now or you're working full-time outside the home, perhaps it's time to

Okay, I admit it. . . .

"I promised myself that I would go to the gym and work out with my free time, but unfortunately for my body, I found that running my errands was way easier to do without buckling and unbuckling two kids numerous times."

—*Danelle, Middleburg Heights, Ohio*

put the "me" back in mommy. And if you manage to make the time to read the rest of this chapter, you'll learn how.

> "With the first four kids, I usually put the others down for naps and had quiet time, but when my last child went to preschool, I ran errands or met friends for lunch!"
>
> *It worked for me!*
>
> —*Stephanie, East Northport, New York*

What About Mom?

NOW THAT YOUR child is in preschool, chances are you're just coming up for air. You survived her diaper days and the sleep deprivation and temper tantrums (hopefully, those are few and far between now). Now that you're less concerned that she'll shove a crayon up your nose when you attempt to read a headline or two in the newspaper, you might get the urge to do something just for you.

Remember you? That nice woman who pretends to be surprised when someone points out you've got grape jelly crusted on your sweatshirt sleeve, even though you were well aware of it when you got dressed this morning?

Having a kid in preschool can open up opportunities for you to get to know yourself again. Now, stop laughing if you've got a baby at home, or twin toddlers, or a baby on the way any second now—or even if you homeschool or work outside the house.

Because having a preschooler can make life easier in all sorts of ways, and not just because there's a chance your kid might not be with you for a few hours each day. As your preschooler becomes more independent, so can you. I'll share some ways to get back to being you after a few years of absence, no matter who you are or what you do.

WE ASKED: How did you spend the hours your child was in preschool?

"I met with friends, cleaned house, ran errands, and spent long showers shaving my legs, exfoliating, and moisturizing without interruption."

—*Stephanie, Hoschton, Georgia*

"I spent some one-on-one time with my youngest, did some shopping, or went to the library with only one kid."

—*Stephanie, St. Paul, Minnesota*

Reclaiming "Me Time"

Let's face it: life isn't about you anymore. Where you used to be the star of your life, lately you've been playing more of a supporting role in someone else's life. And that's okay. That's parenting.

But as your kids get older and more independent, you can—and should—reclaim more time just for yourself. Now, before you dash out to GapKids and call it "me time," think again. While it may feel like a vacation to get your errands done without anyone in tow begging you to let him ride the mall carousel (again), it isn't really recharging, just-for-you downtime. It's just more of the same, minus the kid wrangling. Here are three reasons you should make time for me time:

Okay, I admit it. . . .

"I'm a very involved mommy. A teacher calls, and I spring into action!"

—*Anjanette, Springfield, Illinois*

1. **It'll keep you from burning out.** If you spend all of your time taking care of other people (or taking care of business), you aren't taking care of yourself. Everyone needs time off now and then. Don't feel guilty about it. Feel good that you have the chance in the first place. You deserve it.

2. **It'll make your marriage stronger.** If you're always playing the mommy, you have less of a chance to try to be the wife. "Me time" helps you remember the woman inside the mom, and that's good for Hubby, too. And if you're a single mom, "me time" gives you a chance to get out there a meet someone—also, to shave your legs before your date, which everyone involved will appreciate.

3. **It'll make you happy.** Taking breaks is not only good for you, it's good for your family, because a happy mommy is a good mommy.

Okay, I admit it. . . .

"I attended every preschool function, and I went on every trip."

—*Sherry, Paterson, New Jersey*

Put Down the Glue Gun, and
Put Your Hands Where I Can See Them

ONE OF THE best things about your kids' school years is the chance to volunteer to help out. Also, one of the worst things about your kids' school years is all that volunteering. A serial class mom, I understand the lure of going along on the class trip, the fun of hosting the preschool class party, the appeal of running the fundraiser. But I also know that overvolunteering takes away from any shot you have at some time to yourself. It's true: once you start volunteering, you can get sucked in so deep, it's hard to break free. Here are my top five school volunteering don'ts:

1. **Don't be the first to raise your hand.** You are not the only mom who can bake marshmallow treats or hit up the local pizzeria for a school fundraiser donation. Fly under the radar a little bit, and you'll see that people don't automatically think of you when they think of volunteers. And that will free up your time.

2. **Don't volunteer to do things you hate to do.** If you dislike speaking in front of groups, why would you sign up for PTA president? If you hate crafts, why are you making twenty pilgrim hats for the class Thanksgiving party? Match your desires and abilities to the volunteer job, and you'll not only like it better, it will take up less time, freeing you up to get some of that "me time" you're craving.

3. **Don't make your life way too difficult.** If you've got a baby at home or a full-time job with little flextime, think twice about volunteering for the job that requires you to be in the classroom a lot. Likewise, don't offer to pick up four hundred pumpkins for the school's fall festival if you've got a Volkswagen Beetle and a bad back.

4. **Don't fall prey to the class mom cartel.** You don't need to get together with the three other class moms to flip through the Oriental Trading catalog and decide together on the craft for the class holiday party. Politely suggest that you all trade e-mail addresses, and then do your business online— quickly and efficiently. Delegate the things you hate to do, and stick to what you're best at doing. Soon, you'll find your mornings are free again to go to the gym, catch up on work, or whatever.

5. **Don't get drunk with power.** If you haven't had a pat on the back in a while, the volunteer scene can be alluring, if not intoxicating. Suddenly, people are applauding you—in public! They need you. They rely on you. They depend on you. But they're going to forget about you when the school

Okay, I admit it. . . .

"It's a co-op preschool, so I'm in one or another of their classrooms every five weeks or so. Plus I'm on the board. Actually, I'll be president for the next two years. The first non-U.S. citizen to hold the position. Eat that, Schwarzenegger!"

—*Adam, Allendale, New Jersey*

year ends. Resist the urge to soak up the recognition that volunteering can afford you, because it's only temporary— and it's just preschool.

What to Do with All That Time

So WHAT IF you get that time to yourself and you don't know what to do with it? I've seen it happen. Mom gets a moment, and suddenly, she has no clue what to do, because she hasn't had any "me time" in months, even years. And frankly, it's not like you have an entire day to yourself. Most preschools run about two-and-a-half to three hours at the most. If you subtract the time it takes for you to get there and back, it's even less time. If that time is yours with no little ones in tow, here are a few things you could do:

Okay, I admit it. . . .

"I wasn't involved at all in preschool, because I had baby number two the day after the first day of school."

—*Chrissy, Dillsburg, Pennsylvania*

• Become a home-based shopping party host, selling candles, jewelry, scrapbooking supplies, baskets, or cosmetics

• Blog

• Edit and add music to your home videos

• Get a massage

• Get your hair done without a pint-sized audience hanging at your feet

- Hone your office skills
- Join a bowling league
- Join a gym
- Learn to play an instrument
- Make crafts to give away or sell
- Meet with your girlfriends at a coffee shop (bring back the coffee klatch!)
- Nap
- Network with former coworkers
- Paint or draw
- Read
- Run or jog
- Scrapbook
- Sew, needlepoint, or knit
- Start a business
- Take an online class
- Take karate lessons
- Take tennis or golf lessons
- Take up woodworking, pottery, or floral arranging
- Watch your favorite shows, which you'll tape religiously each week
- Write a book (albeit in tiny chunks at a time)

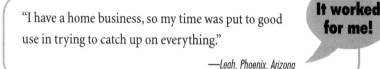

"I have a home business, so my time was put to good use in trying to catch up on everything."

—*Leah, Phoenix, Arizona*

It worked for me!

How to Work from Home Without Losing Your Mind

WHEN MY KIDS were in preschool, I launched MommaSaid.net. Only my kids weren't in school at the same time. One had morning class, and the other was in school afternoons. Ugh! So I found time at night to blog and to teach myself HTML, so I wouldn't have to ask my husband, an IT guy, for help. And I hired a sitter to play with my kids for about ninety minutes each week, so I could get work done. But mostly, I just patched together whatever time I could find to work. I still do, especially during the summer when the kids are home (like I did while writing this book).

If you're thinking of starting your own business at home, or if you're going to work for someone else at your house, you need to keep one major factor in mind: your children don't care if you're working or not. And the younger they are, the harder it is to get anything done at home. But still, it is doable. Here are a few of my top tips for working from home:

1. **Don't think in traditional work days.** Unless you're going to rely on day care or a regular sitter to watch your kids,

you're going to have to steal time to work during nap time, school hours, at night, and so on. This means you might get to work for two hours tomorrow, thirty minutes the next day, and three hours the next. If you think of the thirty-minute work day as a failure, you'll never feel caught up with your work. But if you look at the week as a whole, you'll probably get plenty done—unless everyone's got the flu. Then all bets are off.

2. **Build in plenty of lead time.** Even if you can get a project done for your client by Friday, don't promise it. You never know when a sick kid or a flooded basement will kill your day or days. Always underpromise and overdeliver. Your clients will love you for it.

3. **Outsource as soon as you've got a decent cash flow.** As soon as you can afford to hire out some of the tedious tasks that take time away from your ability to make money, do it. It'll free up your time to get down to the business people pay you for.

4. **Carve out your own space.** I didn't get an office with a door (and a lock) until five years into working at home, but oh how great it is! I find that the kids tend to leave me alone to work more now that I have my own space. Of course, when your kids are very little, you can't let them wander the house unsupervised, so plan out your workspace so that it allows you privacy when you can get it, but keeps you within earshot when you need to be.

5. **Get a phone with a mute button.** You never know when someone will have to go potty right now! Better yet, e-mail whenever possible. Nobody can hear you scream on e-mail.

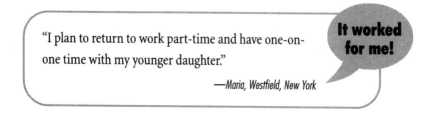

"I plan to return to work part-time and have one-on-one time with my younger daughter."

—*Maria, Westfield, New York*

It worked for me!

Going Back to Work

IF YOU'VE BEEN out of the workforce for a few years, it may seem daunting to try to go back. What do you put on your resume: "Skills: Can simultaneously change a diaper while opening the door for the dog with my foot and cradling the phone"?

Ah, but at-home motherhood does require skills that can be transferred to a paying job. You just have to know how to word it. Here are a few examples to get you started:

• Managed four different schedules at three different schools and numerous extracurricular activities.

• Served as class mom, organizing class trips, parties, and activities

• Oversee household finances, including researching and evaluating investments

- Organized and ran school fundraiser for three years

- Helped raise $10,000 to replace town playground

- Coached kiddie soccer team, teaching twelve four-year-olds the rules of the sport

- Maintain a blog about motherhood that has garnered advertising income and a solid nationwide following

But your cover letter is really what will sell a potential employer on your skills upon returning to the workforce. Make sure you tie in your skills as a mom and volunteer to the job you're applying for. If, for example, you're looking to become an administrative assistant, be sure to play up how you've managed to maintain five people's schedules, all the household bills and tax forms, and so on. If you want to work in a shop, indicate that you were in charge of the school fundraiser's finances, pricing at a garage sale, or a ticket booth at the town carnival. If you want to run the front desk at your gym, show them that you understand how their computer system works, you're familiar with all the trainers' schedules, and so on.

Think about how what you do every day would benefit someone else, and you'll find ways to turn your skills as an at-home mom into a job outside the home.

You Deserve "Me Time" When You Work, Too

SOMETIMES, MOMS WHO work full-time outside the house feel guilty if they're not either working or taking care of their kids. They believe they need to make it up to their kids by spending all their free time with them after work and on weekends. Sometimes, though, they get lost in their well-meaning ways.

If you long for a girls' night out or dinner with Hubby at a restaurant that doesn't supply balloons to patrons, take one now and then. Four or five hours here and there in the grand scheme of your kids' twenty-six-thousand-hour preschool years don't really matter that much. You know you're spending your lunch hours shopping at The Children's Place and hunting down Jimmy Neutron lunch boxes. Ask yourself: Where's my "me time?" And then put it on your calendar. You deserve it!

WE ASKED: What's the best thing about parenting a preschooler?

"They are in school."

—*Sherry, Paterson, New Jersey*

Not "Me Time," but "Mommy and Me Time"

IF YOUR PRESCHOOLER is your oldest child, you're not likely to get much more free time courtesy of preschool. But at least you'll have one fewer kid to wrangle when you're out and about. Plus, you'll get some time to focus on your littler ones. Resist the urge to turn the preschool hours into a variety show, starring you, simply because you feel guilty that your older child had you to himself for a few years before his younger sibling arrived. Chances are, your younger child doesn't know that, and your preschooler doesn't remember it.

Still, it's nice to have something that you do just with your little ones, like a playgroup or a mommy and me-type class—but not every day, and not necessarily the entire school year. I signed my younger son up for Playorama classes, and I took him to a local playgroup now and then.

But when I took him to the supermarket (or to find large pieces of black felt), I didn't feel guilty that I wasn't spending his big brother's school hours entertaining him or preparing him for his preschool days. We spent enough time at the playground after school to make up for all of that, anyhow.

Okay, I admit it. . . .

"She stays at home. Preschool is too expensive!"

—*Beth, Columbia, Maryland*

"I take my older two to the library. We homeschool."

—*Shelley, Travis Air Force Base, California*

It worked for me!

Homeschooling: Not for the Faint of Heart

I'M NOT A homeschooler, no matter what Harry Smith said when I appeared on *The Early Show* to talk about my holiday for at-home moms. (My husband was surprised to hear on national TV that we're homeschooling—me, too.) But if you're homeschooling your kids, I don't have to tell you that you are spending loads of one-on-one (or one-on-two, three, four . . .) time with children. You could use some grown-up time—and I don't mean sharing homeschooling tips with other parents at the playground while the kids play.

Make sure you build in some "me time" so that you're refreshed when you hit the books with the kids. Hey, other teachers get to go home at night. Why shouldn't you get a break, too?

Okay, I admit it. . . .

"Living too far from the school to go home each day, I wander aimlessly around town doing errands, grocery shopping, and generally spending too much money. . . . I do sometimes use the time to go to the library or sit at Starbucks and read a book, but I would really prefer to be able to go home and be productive!"

—*Rebecca, Bluff City, Tennessee*

WE ASKED: What's the best thing about parenting a preschooler?

"Apart from the time I catch up with eighty hours of DVRed shows while they are in class?"

—*Adam, Allendale, New Jersey*

Gimme a break

Think Before You Blog

If you decide to join the ranks of mommy bloggers, be careful. While your preschooler might say and do really funny things right now, eventually, she will be able to Google you and your blog and see what you wrote. Picture her at twelve, thirteen, or older when you decide to post that photo of her wearing nothing but your Tupperware and a smile. Once it's on the Net, it's hard to remove it.

Just a minute!

Five Things *Not* to Do with Your Day Off

Don't . . .

1. See a movie that's animated with talking animals (or chirping robots).

2. Go to a restaurant that provides crayons and a pile of Handi Wipes.

3. Spend your day culling your kids' closets for clothes that no longer fit.

4. Drop by Chuck E. Cheese just because they know you by name.

5. Test the Spanish you learned on *Dora the Explorer*.

Five Things You *Should* Do with Your Day Off

Do . . .

1. Have long, uninterrupted conversations with grown-ups—and *not* about potty training.

2. Read a book that doesn't rhyme.

3. Watch those shows your TV's child blocker filters out.

4. Eat food that doesn't come with a free toy.

5. Shave both legs on the same day.

Chapter Thirteen

But What About . . . ?
Extra Help for Parents of Multiples, Stay-at-Home-Moms, and Other Special Situations

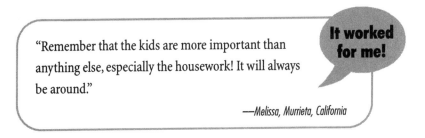

"Remember that the kids are more important than anything else, especially the housework! It will always be around."

It worked for me!

—*Melissa, Murrieta, California*

By the time I was done with the chart, it was clear: it was going to take seven people to replace me. A stay-at-home mom of a toddler and a preschooler, I had to line up a tag team of substitutes, from my husband to my mother to a mom with a big enough car and more folks to fill in for me while I had a same-day laparoscopic surgery for endometriosis, a chronic disease of the pelvis. One person watched my toddler while another took my son to school and still another brought him home. Hubby took me to the hospital and back, and a sitter filled in the gaps. And that was just in the morning.

The combination of stay-at-home motherhood and chronic illness presented issues I wasn't necessarily prepared for handling. So I figured them out along the way. Not all parenting situations are the same. From divorce to parenting multiples to parenting while Daddy is deployed in the armed forces, there are all sorts of situations that make parenting your preschooler all the more challenging. I'll touch on some of the most common situations, some of which I've experienced myself and offer up tips for each.

Okay, I admit it. . . .

"You will constantly second-guess your parenting decisions."

—*Shoshana, Chicago, Illinois*

It worked for me!

"It is critical to schedule some time when you can go out without kids to hang out with family or friends. It is a sort-of sanity-reinforcer when you get to laugh and talk to people who don't have peanut butter smeared on their face."

—*Patricia, West Chester, Pennsylvania*

It worked for me!

"Sometimes, I forget about the laundry, cleaning, and other chores, and put myself first by reading, surfing the net, napping, or watching a little TV. I feel refreshed and ready to get busy again."

—*Kathryn Lufkin, Texas*

Stay-at-Home Motherhood

THERE ARE ABOUT seven million full-time stay-at-home mothers in the United States, but some neighborhoods don't have many of them. As a result, staying home with your kids can be lonely, especially when half the neighbors are at work all day. But it can also be rewarding and fun. It's all how you handle it.

Five Tips for Staying Home with Your Preschooler

1. **Get out!** Chances are you have to leave the house to take your child to preschool. But that's often not enough to stave off the cabin fever that can come with at-home motherhood. Join or organize a playgroup or hang out at the playground where, hopefully, you'll meet other moms. Also, join a mother's group or set up nights out with friends or Hubby, so you can dress up and go somewhere where they don't have ball pits.

2. **Ease up.** Just because you can stay home doesn't mean you have to make every waking moment of your preschooler's life enriching and educational, as though you're preparing him for Yale or Mensa. He needs to learn how to entertain himself, and you need to put down the Millennium Falcon toy and go read a book that has no pictures in it.

3. **Rely on others.** When you're a stay-at-home mom, it's easy to think that everything having to do with the kids or house is solely your job. But staying home with a preschooler can

be long hours of repetitive activities and cleaning up messes. Get your husband to help out as much as possible, and turn to relatives to help entertain or babysit your preschooler, so you can do other things besides parent all the time.

4. **Have something of your own.** If you make every moment of every day all about your preschooler, you'll burn out, and then you'll be no good for anyone, least of all your children. Take up some of those hobbies mentioned in Chapter 12.

5. **Expect more from your preschooler.** As I mentioned in Chapter 11, your preschooler can do more now that she's older. Every now and then, make sure you're not overassisting your preschooler and give her a little more responsibility. Just because you're home with your children doesn't mean you're their personal on-demand life tour guide.

"I make sure that I have activities planned out for chunks of time, so I can at get at least a task or two completed without interruption."

—*Barbara, Arlington, Virginia*

"I try to have activities like drawing that the kids can do right near me."

—*Julie, West Chester, Pennsylvania*

Working from Home

I MENTIONED IN Chapter 12 some tips for working from home without losing your mind. But there's more where that came from. When my kids were in preschool, I learned how to work around their schedules while still getting everything (okay, most of it) done each week.

Five Tips for Working at Home with a Preschooler Underfoot

1. **Be flexible.** You might have big work plans while your preschooler entertains a playdate in the next room. But before you know it, someone stole someone else's Play-Doh, and an argument ensued, and soon, you're playing referee instead of getting work done. Be prepared to shift your work hours to nighttime or weekends when your preschooler's plans for you change.

2. **Get help.** Hire a sitter or trade afternoons with a neighbor who has a preschooler. Put your preschooler in after care if you need the hours. And don't feel guilty about it! Your preschooler will not only adjust, chances are she'll like the change of scenery.

3. **Take work seriously.** Never refer to your job or business as a hobby, even if it doesn't pay much money. The more respect you have for your work, the more your family will help you make sure you have the time to get to your desk.

4. **Spread the word.** You never know if one of your neighbors

could use your services or products, or if they're hiring people to work from home. Make sure you network, even if it's at preschool pick-up, because you could get work out of it.

5. **Prepare for the future.** If you're going to have more hours to work next year when your preschooler hits kindergarten, or if you've decided not to sign up to be class mom in the fall, plan how to best use those hours to work, so they don't get sucked up by running errands or making ghost cupcakes for the mother's group Halloween party.

"I do my best to schedule my over-the-phone interviews during nap times. Sometimes I would pop in a video or turn to Noggin or Sprout and hide in the bedroom closet to get some interviews done. Whatever your job is from home, be flexible."

It worked for me!

—*Apryl, Watkinsville, Georgia*

"Pray. A lot."

—*Melissa, Murrieta, California*

It worked for me!

One Plus One Plus One
Equals Many Preschoolers at Once

THE NATIONAL CENTER for Health Statistics reports that the twin birth rate has risen 55 percent since 1980. And triplets and quadruplets are on the rise, too. But you don't care about everybody else's multiples. Not when you've got two, three, or more outfits to iron for preschool tonight.

I don't have multiples (though I did have two preschoolers at the same time under one roof), so I'll let MommaSaid's moms of multiples supply the tips.

Tips for Parenting Multiple Preschoolers

1. **Don't treat them like a set.** "I have identical twin boys, and I have worked hard to treat them as two boys rather than twins. Let them have their own interests. Take pictures of them together and separate."

   —*Adriann, Toledo, Ohio*

2. **Let them grow at their own rate.** "Try to remember that they are each individuals and have different rates of development. My kids are close in age, and sometimes it can be hard to remember they are not exactly at the same level and reach developments at different times."

   —*Julie, West Chester, Pennsylvania*

3. **Don't referee.** "With twins, it's always like having a playdate in your house, twenty-four hours a day. When my girls

would fight over something, I would automatically take it away and put it on top on the fridge if they couldn't work it out. That way I cut down on the fights."

—*Jill, Kinnelon, New Jersey*

4. **Spend alone time with each one.**
5. **Let them have their own things.** "My kids all have a few things that are theirs only that they don't have to share, including milk cups (by colors), blankets, and stuffed animals. The rest are fair game."

—*Kori, Palmyra, Virginia*

"Have as much communication between him and the kids as possible. Keep pictures around, talk about him all the time, and try not to act anxious. Kids can smell fear!"

It worked for me!

—*Rebecca, Newark, Delaware*

Deployed Daddy

YOUR HUSBAND IS deployed overseas with the military, and you're at home tending to the kids and life and a preschooler who misses his daddy. It's just not the same as having a husband who travels a lot. You're going solo and handling extra issues other moms can't begin to understand. I searched the Internet to find the top tips on handling the stress of parenting while your spouse is deployed.

Five Tips for Holding Down the Fort When Hubby Is Overseas

1. **Skip the war news.** Concentrate on the good news that comes from hearing from your spouse when he calls or e-mails you, rather than watching CNN and wondering if your husband is in harm's way.

2. **Keep Daddy a part of the family.** Let your preschooler talk to her daddy whenever you can. Make videos for your husband to watch, and keep a password-protected blog, so he can see what's new at home when he gets a chance to check a computer. Have your preschooler help you keep a scrapbook about Daddy, and talk about him a lot. A few months is a very long time in the life of a preschooler, so it's important to keep Daddy in the forefront whenever possible.

3. **Keep in touch.** If your husband's schedule permits it, try to set up a regular time to talk, and make a big deal out of it when he calls. Your preschooler will love to celebrate whenever Daddy calls.

4. **Expect issues.** Your preschooler may become emotionally withdrawn or visibly sad after your husband leaves for his tour of duty. Expect separation anxiety and other emotional issues, and don't dismiss them. Encourage your preschooler to share her feelings, and keep as busy as possible. If your preschooler's emotional response gets too much for you to handle, seek professional help.

5. **Don't show your fear.** Your preschooler is too young to understand that Daddy might be in harm's way. Save your sad feelings for adults who can help you work through your emotions.

"Don't be surprised if the homecoming reaction isn't the best. It's hard for the kids to emotionally process a parent being gone, so keep showing them that you love them even if they seem unhappy. They really do care and haven't developed the right skills yet."

It worked for me!

—*Julie, West Chester, Pennsylvania*

Single Moms

THE CENSUS BUREAU states that a quarter of all children under twenty-one live with a single parent—more than 80 percent of which are mothers. Certainly, you're not alone if you are separated, divorced, or even widowed, though you might feel like it. If your husband travels a lot, you can feel like a single mom much of the time. Explaining to a preschooler why Daddy is gone is complicated and difficult. I've searched for some of the best tips for handling the situation.

Five Tips for Parenting a Preschooler After Divorce

1. **Don't dis Daddy.** Even if your ex has gone and done something stupid or otherwise made it impossible for you to, say, pay for preschool, keep it to yourself. As hard as it is to

bite your tongue, it's the best thing for your preschooler.

2. **Try to limit change.** The less you can keep your preschooler's life from turning upside down, the easier the change will be on him. If possible, keep his school the same, at least until the summer.

3. **Don't break the rules.** Even if Daddy is buying him electronic mini-Jeeps to drive through your flowers and taking him on trips to Disneyland, resist the urge to counteroffer by spoiling your preschooler. He needs structure and boundaries just as much now as he did before the divorce.

4. **Don't ask your preschooler to play favorites.** It isn't fair to your child to make her pick you over your ex for anything, including visitation schedules and love. Let her treat the both of you the way she wants to.

5. **Don't sweat the small stuff.** If your ex calls from the ice cream shop to say he'll be late dropping off your preschooler, don't make a big deal about it. You don't need to turn every little transgression into a battle zone. The more flexible you are about the small stuff, the better it is for your preschooler.

When Daddy Is Away

My mother says that my father traveled two weeks out of every month when I was little. And yet, I remember Dad sitting along

> "We always talk to Daddy at least once a day when he travels. Using bedtime to talk about the day and say good-nights is a must!"
>
> **It worked for me!**
>
> — *Melissa, Murrieta, California*

the sidelines of my Saturday morning soccer games, and I remember dancing with him at the Girl Scouts's Father-Daughter Square Dance. Somehow, I remember that he was there, even if he wasn't around as often as some other dads were. If your husband travels a lot, here are some pointers on making it work for your family:

Five Tips for When Daddy Travels Often

1. **Tape it.** If Daddy is missing the holiday play at the preschool or even just a fun evening at the ice cream shop, videotape it, and send him the file. Or wait until he comes home and then share it with him and your preschooler, so he can feel a part of it. Even if he can't be there in person, he can be there in spirit.

2. **Map it.** Use a globe or a map to show your preschooler where Daddy is traveling. If he's got a lot of stops in many cities, it will be fun for your preschooler to map them out—with your help, of course. Daddy could also bring home a small souvenir, like a magnet, from each city he visits. That way, your preschooler gets a treat whenever Daddy comes home and a nice collection to treasure.

3. **Share it.** Try to talk to Daddy at least once a day. Allow your preschooler to share one thing in each call, even if she simply

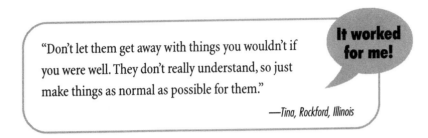

"Don't let them get away with things you wouldn't if you were well. They don't really understand, so just make things as normal as possible for them."

—Tina, Rockford, Illinois

rambles on about what happened on *Dora the Explorer* that day. It'll help them stay connected if they get to hear each other's voices, and you'll get a mini-break from all things Dora.

4. **Treat them.** If Daddy can save up enough frequent flyer miles, he can treat the family to a short trip that everyone will enjoy. Make sure you explain to your preschooler that Daddy's work made your trip possible, so he understands that there are benefits to all that traveling—besides the free souvenirs.

5. **Watch your tongue.** Don't call yourself a "single mother," even if you feel like one when Daddy is away. Make sure you show your preschooler that Dad is an important part of your family by talking him up whether he's in a conference room in Brussels, at a truck stop on I-95, or in the next room.

It worked for me!

"My best advice is to reach out and ask for help, you'll be amazed at how willing people are to help. Also, tell your children the truth and include them. My five-year-old daughter watched me get radiation, and that helped alleviate her fears."

—Jennifer, Erie, Pennsylvania

Gimme a break

Don't Hide It from the Kids

If you have cancer, tell your kids. It's better for them to hear it from you than to overhear it at school or when you're on the phone. Use stuffed animals, dolls, or books to explain what cancer means. Tell them what to expect about their schedules and daily routines. Assure them they didn't cause the cancer and—this one's very important at this age—that they can't catch it. The more selectively honest you are, the better it is for your children in the long run.

Ill Mommy

I'm not talking about the flu here; I'm talking about the chronic, the deadly, and the debilitating. I've parented through chronic pain from endometriosis and lymphoma, so I know firsthand how hard it can be when you're a chronically ill mother. Here are a few pointers.

Five Tips for Parenting a Preschooler when You're Chronically Ill

1. **Surrender to the new you.** If you're too sick to parent like you used to, remember this: that's okay. Don't beat yourself up because you're not as strong as you used to be. This is no time to try to be Super Mom, especially if it makes you sicker. It's time to parent in a whole new way—a way that works for you, your health, and your preschooler.

2. **Ask for help.** I learned that when you're seriously ill, people want to help. Don't be afraid to ask for it. If people want to shop for you, drive carpool to preschool, or bring you dinners, let them. The less you have to do, the more energy you'll have for your preschooler.

3. **Keep the affection coming.** Your preschooler needs lots of hugs and kisses right now, and so do you. Showing affection to your preschooler helps reassure her that Mommy's still Mommy, even if she's in her pj's all day nowadays or commuting to the hospital.

4. **Save your energy.** If your preschooler knows your illness keeps her home, she'll start to resent it. So save up your strength for when you really need it. If you're feeling really good one day, treat your preschooler to a trip to the playground or Chuck E. Cheese—whatever you (and your immune system) can handle.

5. **Shower him with attention.** You don't have to run the Halloween parade to be a good mom. Your preschooler just wants your time and attention. Play quiet games or watch a video while snuggling on the couch.

Which One of These Is Not Like the Others?

WHATEVER YOUR SPECIAL situation, seek out other people who are going through or who have been through the same thing as you.

You'll feel much better when you can share your concerns and issues with someone who truly understands what it's like to be in your shoes. On the Internet, you'll find websites that offer support both online and in person, and there are lots of books about your specific issue on the shelves at your library or local bookstores. If you need one-on-one help with a serious issue, consider seeing a trained counselor. Whatever you do, remember that your preschooler loves you no matter what.

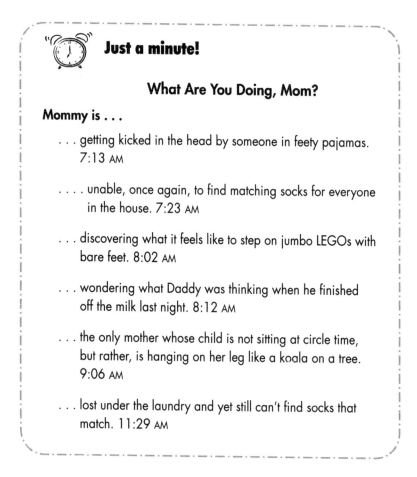

Just a minute!

What Are You Doing, Mom?

Mommy is . . .

...getting kicked in the head by someone in feety pajamas. 7:13 AM

....unable, once again, to find matching socks for everyone in the house. 7:23 AM

...discovering what it feels like to step on jumbo LEGOs with bare feet. 8:02 AM

...wondering what Daddy was thinking when he finished off the milk last night. 8:12 AM

...the only mother whose child is not sitting at circle time, but rather, is hanging on her leg like a koala on a tree. 9:06 AM

...lost under the laundry and yet still can't find socks that match. 11:29 AM

. . . heading back to the preschool, even though it feels like she just left there. 11:44 AM

. . . trying to avoid the class mom, who needs someone to bake two dozen cupcakes by tomorrow. 12:06 PM

. . . just getting some milk . . . and gummy bears, rainbow sprinkles, and a package of plastic goody bag whistles, just to keep the peace. 12:59 PM

. . . standing over the sink, finishing off the chicken nuggets. Again. 1:13 PM

. . . a huge fan of nap time and misses it terribly. 1:28 PM

. . . pretending she has no clue why the battery-operated Elmo doll can't sing anymore. 3:18 PM

. . . glad she only needs one hand to operate the microwave. 5:59 PM

. . . hiding the milk in the back of the fridge this time. 7:47 PM

. . . making two dozen cupcakes for school. 7:59 PM

. . . a sucker. 8:01 PM

. . . making room in bed for those squirmy feety pajamas. 8:48 PM

Bye-Bye!

So there you have it—everything I'd tell you about preschoolers if we had a few hours and a whole lotta coffee together. But let's face it: you'd have to dash off for preschool pick-up, anyhow.

There's other stuff you'll learn along the way, but I wanted to give you the big picture in a way that you may not have seen before. It's like we met at the proverbial back fence and, mom-to-mom, went through all the things that keep us up at night when it comes to preschoolers, from finding the right school to teaching independence to trying to figure out why trees aren't purple.

You might have a different experience with certain aspects of raising preschoolers, and you'll no doubt have your own advice to give. Share it with friends who have preschoolers now or whose

Okay, I admit it. . . .

"I love seeing life through their eyes. It's so simple and really how it should be."

—*Kristina, Marysville, Ohio*

toddlers are about to reach their third birthday, because we moms should help each other out— especially when our preschoolers are questioning our every move.

Whether every word in this book was eye-opening or simply a reassuring pat on the back, remember one very important thing while you're parenting preschoolers: you're not the only one going through it, no matter how lonely it feels at times. Whenever you need a pick-me-up, flip through this guide, or drop by Momma-Said.net for a laugh and some validation. You know, just as soon as you look up why penguins can't fly and whether it's possible to travel to the moon by Tuesday.

—*Jen Singer*

WE ASKED: So far, what have been the favorite years of your kids' lives?

Babies (up to 1): 9%
Toddlers (1-3): 13%
The preschool years: 43%
Grade-schoolers (5-7) 6%
Tweens (8 - 12): 2%
Teens 0%
Not sure: 17 %
No opinion 11%

Just a minute!

Preschool Years Exit Interview

1. What is your primary reason for leaving?

   My kid starts kindergarten tomorrow. Besides, I've already been snagged to serve as class mom this year, and I've got twenty Oriental Trading catalogs to go through.

2. Did anything trigger your decision to leave?

   Yes, I finally stopped watching videos of my child at pre-school graduation singing, "I Believe I Can Fly" while I sobbed uncontrollably.

3. What was most satisfying part of the preschool years?

   When my child decided to finish potty training the day before school started.

4. What was the least satisfying part of the preschool years?

   When he regressed a month later after the baby was born.

5. Did your duties turn out as you expected?

   If somebody had told me that I'd learn how to race through Kohl's, Target, the post office, and the supermarket and still make it back to preschool pick-up with a minute to spare, I wouldn't have believed it, anyhow.

6. Did you receive enough training to do your job well?

   Exactly how do you train for rescuing the guinea pig from a playdate pal who just wanted to see if it could outrun the cat?

7. Did you receive adequate feedback about your performance?

   That's what necklaces made from Fruit Loops are for.

8. Did you find opportunities to advance?

> Well, I did move up to head class mom this year, and my sister-in-law keeps calling me for advice on everything from cradle cap to umbilical cord stumps.

9. Were your coworkers helpful?

> If it weren't for my husband, my preschooler wouldn't have a bed frame shaped like Cinderella's castle and the ability to burp the Barney "I Love You" song.

10. Can we do anything to encourage you to stay?

> *Nope. It's time for kindergarten. Besides, we've already signed up for the kindergarten soccer clinic, and I'm in charge of the Gatorade. Is Costco still open?*

Index

About the Author

Jen Singer is the creator of MommaSaid.net, a Forbes Best of the Web community for moms. She is the author of the Stop Second-Guessing Yourself parenting series, *You're a Good Mom (and Your Kids Aren't So Bad Either)* and *14 Hours 'Til Bedtime: A Stay-at-Home Mom's Life in 27 Funny Little Stories.*

Jen writes the Good Grief! blog about parenting tweens for goodhousekeeping.com, which is syndicated on Yahoo! Shine. She is the creator of "*Please* Take My Children to Work Day," a holiday for stay-at-home moms celebrated on the last Monday each June which has been officially proclaimed by governors in a dozen states so far.

Jen's humor has appeared in *American Baby, Family Circle, New York Times, Parenting, Parents, Woman's Day* and *Chicken Soup for Every Mom's Soul.* She was named a Swiffer Amazing Woman of the Year. She is a spokesperson for several major corporations. She has appeared on ABC's *World News Now, NBC News,* CBS's *The Early Show, CBS Evening News,* Parents TV, numerous local news programs along the East Coast, as well as several Canadian TV shows and dozens of radio programs, including Sally Jessy Raphael's Talk Net and XM's Take Five.

A soccer coach, class mom and cancer survivor, she lives in northern New Jersey with her husband and two sons, who leave various rolling objects on the floor of her mini van for her to discover whenever she hits the breaks.